Guide to

Carav
&Camp ...g
Holidays 2005

GW00703220

England, Scotland, Wales & Ireland

with

Caravan Sites, Holiday Parks and Centres
Caravans for Hire, Camping Sites

For **Contents** see Page 3
For **Index** of towns/counties see back of book

FHG Publications
Paisley

COUNTRY
&LEISURE Part of IPC Country and Leisure Media
—MEDIA—

CONTENTS

Guide to CARAVAN & CAMPING HOLIDAYS 2005

ENGLAND

SCOTLAND

WALES

NORTHERN IRELAND

REPUBLIC OF IRELAND

ENGLAND and WALES Counties

NORTH WALES
1. Denbighshire
2. Flintshire
3. Wrexham

SOUTH WALES
4. Swansea
5. Neath and Port Talbot
6. Bridgend
7. Rhondda Cynon Taff
8. Merthyr Tydfil
9. Vale of Glamorgan
10. Cardiff
11. Caerphilly
12. Blaenau Gwent
13. Torfaen
14. Newport
15. Monmouthshire

NORTHUMBERLAND

TYNE & WEAR

DURHAM

CUMBRIA

ISLE OF MAN

NORTH YORKSHIRE

LANCASHIRE

WEST YORKSHIRE

EAST RIDING OF YORKSHIRE

GREATER MANCHESTER

MERSEYSIDE

SOUTH YORKSHIRE

ISLE OF ANGLESEY

CONWY

CHESHIRE

DERBYSHIRE

LINCOLNSHIRE

NOTTINGHAM-SHIRE

GWYNEDD

STAFFORDSHIRE

SHROPSHIRE

LEICESTERSHIRE

RUTLAND

NORFOLK

WEST MIDLANDS

POWYS

CAMBRIDGESHIRE

CEREDIGION

WARWICKSHIRE

NORTHAMPTONSHIRE

WORCESTERSHIRE

SUFFOLK

HEREFORDSHIRE

BEDFORDSHIRE

PEMBROKESHIRE

CARMARTHENSHIRE

GLOUCESTERSHIRE

BUCKINGHAM-SHIRE

HERTFORDSHIRE

ESSEX

OXFORDSHIRE

BRISTOL

BERKSHIRE

GREATER LONDON

WILTSHIRE

SURREY

KENT

SOMERSET

HAMPSHIRE

WEST SUSSEX

E. SUSSEX

DEVON

DORSET

ISLE OF WIGHT

CORNWALL

SCILLY ISLES

©MAPS IN MINUTES™ 2004

20 award winning holiday parks

in Cornwall, Devon, Dorset, Norfolk, Wales, & Scotland

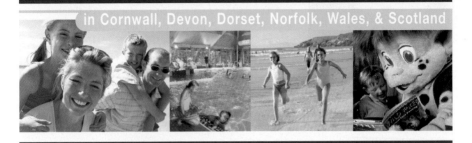

Grannie's Heilan' Hame

Nairn Lochloy

Tummel Valley

Wemyss Bay NEW!

Sundrum Castle

Southerness NEW!

Cherry Tree NEW!

Pendine Sands NEW!

Trecco Bay

Ruda

St Minver

West Bay

Warmwell NEW!

Newquay
White Acres
Crantock Beach
Holywell Bay

Torquay NEW!

Challaborough Bay

Sea Acres

★ Kid's and Teen's clubs

★ Adventure play areas

★ Indoor & Outdoor pools with waterslides

★ Live family entertainment, bars & food

★ A choice of accommodation
including caravans & lodges
with double glazing and
central heating

★ Touring & camping pitches
with excellent facilities

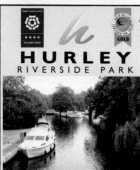

A family-run caravan and campsite renowned for its cleanliness and hospitality, situated on the coastal route between Tintagel and Boscastle in the historically interesting hamlet of Bossiney. Bossiney is ideally situated to enjoy the breathtaking beauty of the Cornish Coast, with Bossiney Cove, a safe, sandy bay, a short walk away. Bossiney Farm is a terraced park, giving our 20 static caravans an individual rural view. There is a range of modern luxury caravan homes (some new for 2005), offering a choice of length, width and bedroom layouts – to suit all needs, with a well equipped kitchen and everything you would expect on a modern caravan holiday.

We have touring and camping pitches, many with electric hook-ups. The site is landscaped with flat, sheltered terraces, and serviced by tarmac and concrete roads. Well appointed, bright and clean toilet block, with showers, hairdryers (token) and free hot water to handbasins and wash sinks. We have a well stocked shop, laundry and baby changing and disabled facilities. PETS WELCOME.

How to find us
Conveniently situated on the B3263, between Tintagel and Boscastle, we are in an ideal position for touring all of Cornwall, and much of Devon, is within easy reach.

Bossiney Farm Caravan & Camping Park
Tintagel, Cornwall PL34 0AY

TEL: 01840 770481 • FAX: 01840 770025
www.bossineyfarm.co.uk

Gunvenna Touring Caravan and Camping Park

The Park is a well-drained site of level grassland on 10 acres commanding uninterrupted views of the countryside within five minutes' drive of safe golden sandy beaches. Local activities include golf, fishing, tennis, surfing and swimming, etc. Site facilities include two modern toilet and shower blocks, launderette and ironing room, children's play area, children's games room (9am to 10pm), barbecue area, dog exercise area, shop, telephone, etc. We also have a licensed bar and a indoor heated swimming pool. Please send for our colour brochure and tariff.

AA

RAC Listed

St Minver, Wadebridge PL27 6QN
Tel: 01208 862405

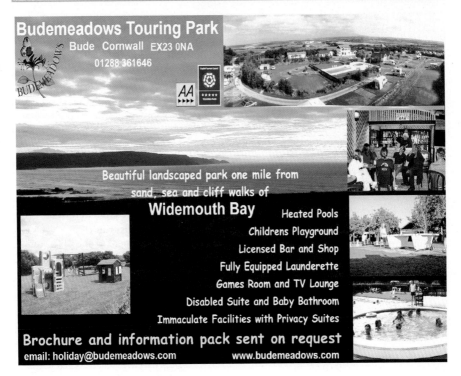

Budemeadows Touring Park

Bude Cornwall EX23 0NA
01288 361646

AA
★★★★★
TOURING PARK

Beautiful landscaped park one mile from
sand, sea and cliff walks of
Widemouth Bay

Heated Pools
Childrens Playground
Licensed Bar and Shop
Fully Equipped Launderette
Games Room and TV Lounge
Disabled Suite and Baby Bathroom
Immaculate Facilities with Privacy Suites

Brochure and information pack sent on request
email: holiday@budemeadows.com www.budemeadows.com

Globe Vale Holiday Park
Radnor, Redruth, Cornwall TR16 4BH

Globe Vale is a quiet countryside park situated close to the town of Redruth and the main A30. There are panoramic views across green fields to the coast; 10 minutes' drive to the nearest beach. Campers/tourers; static caravans for hire, and also plots available if you wish to buy your own new static holiday home.
Facilities on site include electric hook-ups, shower/toilet block, launderette and sluice. There is also a children's play area, and open spaces for ball games. We are happy to accept pets on site at extra charge.

Contact Paul and Louise Owen on 01209 891183 • www.globevale.co.uk

Greenhowe Caravan Park
Great Langdale, English Lakeland.

Greenhowe is a permanent Caravan Park with Self Contained Holiday Accommodation. Subject to availability Holiday Homes may be rented for short or long periods from 1st March until mid-November. The Park is situated in the heart of the Lake District some half a mile from Dungeon Ghyll at the foot of the Langdale Pikes. It is an ideal centre for Climbing, Fell Walking, Riding, Swimming, Water Skiing or just a lazy holiday.

Please ask about Short Breaks

Greenhowe Caravan Park
Great Langdale, Ambleside
Cumbria LA22 9JU

For free colour brochure
Telephone: (015394) 37231
Fax: (015394) 37464
Freephone: 0800 0717231
www.greenhowe.com

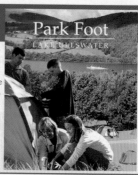

NEWHAVEN

Caravan & Camping Park

Delightful site in the heart of the Peak District providing an ideal centre for touring the Derbyshire Dales, walking, climbing, potholing, etc. Convenient for visiting Chatsworth, Haddon House, Hardwick House, Alton Towers, Matlock and the Dams. Two first class toilet blocks providing FREE hot water; electric hook-ups. Children's playground, playroom, fully-stocked shop supplying Calor and Camping gas, fresh groceries, etc. Laundry. Ice pack freezing facilities. Restaurant adjacent. Tents, motor vans, caravans. Pets and children welcome.

Newhaven Caravan and Camping Park, Newhaven, Near Buxton, Derbyshire SK17 0DT (01298 84300)

Terms from £8.50 per night – includes car and up to four people, discount for seven nights or more. SAE for brochure. Seasonal tourers welcome.

Holmans Wood
Holiday Park

Delightful, personally managed Park set back in secluded wooded area. Easily accessed from the A38 and ideally situated for Dartmoor and Haldon Forest. Close to Exeter, Plymouth and Torquay, and sandy beaches at Dawlish and Teignmouth. Trout and coarse fishing, golf, horse riding and bird watching are near by.

Our facilities: • Some hardstandings • Electric hook-ups •Excellent toilets/showers • Disabled toilet •Meadow for camping
Seasonal pitches • Storage available • Holiday homes for sale •Rallies welcome • Credit card facility for telephone bookings

Chudleigh, Devon TQ13 0DZ • Tel: 01626 853785 • Fax: 01626 853792
e-mail: enquiries@holmanswood.co.uk • website: www.holmanswood.co.uk

---

Mounts Farm Touring Park
The Mounts, Near East Allington, Kingsbridge TQ9 7QJ • 01548 521591

MOUNTS FARM is a family-run site in the heart of South Devon. On-site facilities include FREE hot showers, flush toilets, FREE hot water in washing-up room, razor points, laundry and information room, electric hook-ups and site shop. We welcome tents, touring caravans and motor caravans. Large pitches in level, sheltered fields. No charges for awnings. Children and pets welcome. Situated three miles north of Kingsbridge, Mounts Farm is an ideal base for exploring Dartmouth, Salcombe, Totnes, Dartmoor and the many safe, sandy beaches nearby.

www.mountsfarm.co.uk • Self-catering cottage also available.

Axevale Caravan Park
Colyford Road, Seaton EX12 2DF • Tel: 0800 0688816

A quiet, family-run park with 68 modern and luxury caravans for hire. The park overlooks the delightful River Axe Valley, and is just a 10 minute walk from the town with its wonderfully long, award-winning beach. Children will love our extensive play area, with its sand pit, paddling pool, swings and slide. Laundry facilities are provided and there is a wide selection of goods on sale in the park shop which is open every day. All of our caravans have a shower, toilet, fridge and TV. Also, with no clubhouse, a relaxing atmosphere is ensured. Prices from £80 per week; reductions for three or fewer persons early/late season.

website: www.axevale.co.uk

EUROPA PARK

Beach Road, Woolacombe
North Devon, EX34 7AN
Bookings: 01271 871425

Early Bookings 10% Discount!

www.europapark.co.uk

Camping and Touring
We have beautiful landscaped Camping and Touring pitches, all overlooking Woolacombe Beach & Lundy Island. Electric Pitches and All Service pitches are available.

Site Accommodation
Luxury wooden lodges, Bungalows, Static Caravans, Cabins & Chalets available sleeping from 4 - 8 people.

Facilities
Restaurant, Clubhouse, Indoor Swimming Pool, Sauna, Launderette, SPAR④ Market.

Special Area - For Young People & Large Groups. *Open All Year!*

Best Views in Woolacombe - "Probably!"

The Camping and Caravanning Club

The nearest camping and caravan park to the sea, in perfectly secluded beautiful coastal country. Our family-run park, adjoining National Trust land, is only 500 yards from Rockham Beach, yet only five

North Morte Farm Caravan & Camping, Dept. FHG, Mortehoe, Woolacombe EX34 7EG (01271 870381)

minutes' walk from the village of Mortehoe with a Post Office, petrol station/garage, shops, cafes and pubs – one of which has a children's room. Four to six berth holiday caravans for hire and pitches for tents, dormobiles and touring caravans, electric hook-ups available. We have hot showers and flush toilets, laundry room, shop and off-licence; Calor gas and Camping Gaz available; children's play area. Dogs accepted but must be kept on lead. Open Easter to end September. Brochure available.

★★★★
HOLIDAY PARK

HARFORD BRIDGE HOLIDAY PARK

Peter Tavy, Tavistock, Devon PL19 9LS
Tel: 01822 810349 • Fax: 01822 810028
www.harfordbridge.co.uk
E-mail: enquiry@harfordbridge.co.uk

Rose award park

Beautiful sheltered park set in Dartmoor beside the River Tavy with delightful views of the moor. Riverside camping and other level pitches. Luxury self-catering caravan holiday homes open all year. Off the A386 Okehampton Road, two miles from Tavistock. Take Peter Tavy turning.

GOLD

★★★★
HOLIDAY PARK

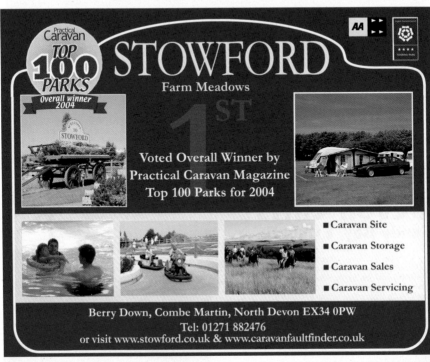

REDLANDS FARM CARAVAN PARK

...for Personal Service
and Easiest Access to
Weymouth Beach...

Very conveniently situated in a semi-rural location backing onto open fields, yet not too far from the town centre and 1½ miles from the seafront. Buses stop just outside the park entrance and serve not only the town centre but much of Dorset. Ideal for day trips exploring the lovely countryside.

* Thirty 4 - 8 berth modern luxury caravans for hire with all services plus colour TV and fridge * Friendly family-run park * Launderette facilities * Supermarkets close by * Personal supervision * Caravan sales * Children and Pets welcome * Plenty of official footpaths and country walks to explore * Car parking alongside caravans * Open March to October * Terms per week £150 - £440

SAE for enquiries.

REDLANDS FARM CARAVAN PARK

DORCHESTER ROAD, WEYMOUTH, DORSET DT3 5AP
Tel: 01305 812291 • Fax: 01305 814251

Redlands Sports Club is opposite the park where club, bar and sports facilities are available. Membership open to all visitors.

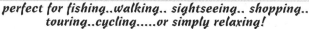

Rowan Leisure Holidays

luxury caravan holidays in Norfolk
www.rowanleisureholidays.co.uk

HAVEN, CAISTER-ON-SEA • Gold & Silver
3-bedroom static caravans (2003 models)
CALIFORNIA CLIFFS, SCRATBY • **Bronze 3-bedroom caravan**
All caravans on both sites have a modern shower, WC, oven, fridge,
microwave, heater, DVD/TV, comfortably sized lounge and modern kitchen.
• All rentals include electricity, gas, heating and hot water
• Laundered bed linen and towels • Fire extinguisher and smoke detector
• All caravans have had the relevant safety checks.
*Both holiday camps have on site amenities such as a night club, swimming pool, children's activities,
and cabaret acts. Both sites have sandy beaches and excellent family facilities.*
For information and bookings please telephone 01263 825333
e-mail: enquiries@rowanleisureholidays.co.uk

For premier touring in Great Yarmouth

PARK FACILITIES
Over 220 all electric sites
Awnings FREE
Grass & hard standings
Modern heated shower & toilet
blocks
Free car parking
Gas cylinder refills on site
Night security for late arrivals
Hair dryers
Baby changing facilities
New Super Pitch
Full mains service pitch with hedged,
landscaped and awning areas

GREAT YARMOUTH
No.1 Holiday Park
Vauxhall
HOLIDAY PARK 2005

FREE WITH YOUR HOLIDAY
Star Studded Entertainment
Indoor Tropical Waterworld
New Splash Zone
Sport & Fitness Fun
Kid's Club and Nursery
Satellite T.V. (super pitch only)
Electricity

Call Now For a Free Brochure
01493 857231
91 Acle New Road Great Yarmouth Norfolk NR30 1TB Ref: 91
www.vauxhall-holiday-park.co.uk

Golden Beach Holiday Centre
– for a family holiday

**National Caravan
Council Member**

**Open March 22nd
to October 31st**

The Golden Beach Holiday Centre nestles beneath a bank
of dunes, beyond which are some of the finest sands in
East Anglia. We know just how important your family
holiday is for you and and in a luxurious holiday home at
the Golden Beach Centre, with its full on-site facilities,
relaxation and enjoyment are assured.
• Luxury holiday homes to rent or for sale • On-site shop
• Restaurant, Bar • Launderette • Children's play area
• Shower rooms and toilet facilities • Mains electricity
• Perfect centre for exploring Norfolk and The Broads

Golden Beach Holiday Centre
Beach Road • Sea Palling • Norfolk NR12 0AL
Tel: 01692 598269 • Fax: 01692 598693

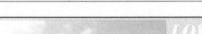
LOWE CARAVAN PARK

SMALL FRIENDLY COUNTRY PARK.

Primarily a touring park, we now have four
luxury holiday homes for hire in peaceful
surroundings, ideal for touring East Anglia
or a quiet relaxing break. More suited to
over 50s, but children are welcome.

Tel: 01953 881051
May Lowe, Ashdale, Hills Road, Saham Hills
(Near Watton), Thetford, Norfolk IP25 7EZ

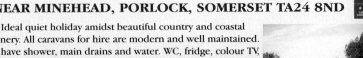

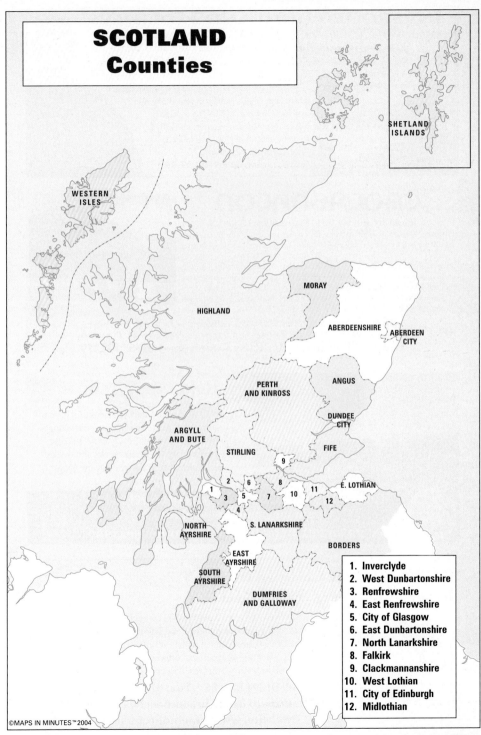

SCOTLAND
Counties

SHETLAND ISLANDS

WESTERN ISLES

HIGHLAND

MORAY

ABERDEENSHIRE

ABERDEEN CITY

PERTH AND KINROSS

ANGUS

DUNDEE CITY

ARGYLL AND BUTE

STIRLING

FIFE

9

2   6   8

1   10   11   E. LOTHIAN

3   5   7   12

4

NORTH AYRSHIRE

S. LANARKSHIRE

EAST AYRSHIRE

BORDERS

SOUTH AYRSHIRE

DUMFRIES AND GALLOWAY

1. Inverclyde
2. West Dunbartonshire
3. Renfrewshire
4. East Renfrewshire
5. City of Glasgow
6. East Dunbartonshire
7. North Lanarkshire
8. Falkirk
9. Clackmannanshire
10. West Lothian
11. City of Edinburgh
12. Midlothian

ROSNEATH CASTLE PARK
SO NEAR... YET SO FAR AWAY

Rosneath Castle Park has everything to offer if you are looking for a touring or camping holiday. No more than an hour's drive from Glasgow, the 57 acres that the park occupies along the shore of Gareloch offers the perfect opportunity to relax and discover another world, and another you.

Thistle Awarded Luxury Self-Catering Holiday Homes with superb views. In a beautiful setting with first class facilities including an adventure playground, boat house, fun club, restaurant and bar, there's no end to the reasons why you would 'wish you were here'.

Rosneath Castle Park, Rosneath,
Near Helensburgh, Argyll G84 0QS
Tel: (01436) 831208
Fax: (01436) 831978
E Mail: enquiries@rosneathcastle.demon.co.uk
Website: www.rosneathcastle.demon.co.uk

Coastal Snowdonia
300 YARDS FROM LONG SANDY BEACH

ENJOY THE BEST OF BOTH WORLDS, BETWEEN SEA AND MOUNTAINS

A 'DRAGON AWARD' PARK BY THE WALES TOURIST BOARD FOR HIGH STANDARDS AND FACILITIES

Luxury Holiday Homes For Hire. All with Shower, Toilet, Fridge, Colour TV and Continental Quilts.

- **Licensed Clubhouse**
- **Entertainment**
- **Heated Swimming Pool**
- **Games Room**
- **Tourers & Campers on level grassland**
- **Electrical Hook-ups available**
- **Flush Toilets, Hot Showers**
- **Washing-up facilities**
- **Children's Play Area**
- **Launderette**

• Pets Welcome under control

For Colour Brochure, write or telephone

Dinlle Caravan Park, Dinas Dinlle, Caernarfon LL54 5TS
Tel: 01286 830324
www.thornleyleisure.co.uk

HENDRE MYNACH TOURING CARAVAN AND CAMPING PARK
SITUATED IN SOUTHERN SNOWDONIA

Close to the beautiful Mawddach Estuary. 100 yards from safe sandy beach. Excellent base for walking and cycling, close to Cycle Route 8. All modern amenities. Hard standings available. Pets welcome, dog walk on site. Approximately 20 minutes pleasant walk along promenade to Barmouth town centre. Bus service and train station close by.

Open 1st March - 9th January
SPECIAL OFFERS AVAILABLE SPRING & AUTUMN
PHONE FOR COLOUR BROCHURE
Barmouth, Gwynedd, LL42 1YR
Tel: 01341 280262
www.hendremynach.co.uk • E-mail: mynach@lineone.net

"AA BEST CAMPSITE IN WALES 2001"

Tyn Rhôs Camping Site   Tel: 01407 860369

A long established camping and touring site. Hot showers, toilets, chemical disposal, electric hook-ups etc. Separate rally field available. Rural location within walking distance of beautiful seaside resort. Perfect for out of season tranquillity, weekend breaks or family holidays. With bathing, sailing, fishing, diving, horse riding, golf, birdwatching, climbing, walking etc nearby, there's something for everyone, even a day trip to Ireland!

A55 across Anglesey, Junction 3 to Valley, left at traffic lights onto B4545 for Trearddur Bay. Turn left onto Ravenspoint Road. One mile to shared entrance, take left branch.

★★

Ravenspoint Road, Trearddur Bay, Holyhead, Isle of Anglesey LL65 2AX

Islawrffordd Caravan Park
Tal-y-Bont, Merioneth LL43 2BQ

Situated on the Snowdonia coastline, just north of Barmouth, our park offers a limited number of caravans for hire, most of which come with double glazing and central heating along with laundered bedding. Our touring caravan field has been modernised to super pitch quality including hard standing with each plot being reservable. Camping is also available on a first-come, first-served basis.

Park facilities include • shop • laundry • indoor heated pool • bar • amusements • food bars. Enquiries regarding any of the above to **John or Jane**.

Tel: 01341 247269 • Fax: 01341 242639
e-mail: info@islawrffordd.co.uk • website: www.islawrffordd.co.uk

Pitton Cross
Caravan & Camping Park
The family friendly park

Pitton Cross Caravan & Camping Park
Rhossili, Swansea SA3 1PH
Tel: 01792 390 593 • Fax: 01792 391 010

Close to the village of Rhossili, comprising six level paddocks each with 15-20 pitches, some with sea views, others offering peace and privacy. Convenient water and hook-up points. 'Dog free' and 'families only' areas. Clean modern shower and utility block, dish washing area, laundry room, parent and toddler room with baby bath and changing facilities. On-site shop for food and other essentials. Breathtaking coastal scenery, unrivalled countryside and fabulous sunsets. Walking, water sports, rock climbing, cycling.

See our kite centre for an extensive range of kites.
Also fishing tackle and a selection of gifts and crafts.

www.pittoncross.co.uk

Sports and Leisure

We have horse riding facilities on the site together with beach donkeys that work regularly depending on the tide and weather. Immediately adjacent to the site there are tennis courts and a bowling green. There is also a golf course within two miles. A particular feature of the site is that whilst having the benefits of the village on one side, it has an attractive cliff path for walkers between the site and sea that stretches for miles. It is the intention of the local council to extend this walk right around the island.

The Site.....

There are a number of flush toilet blocks together with two shower blocks. Mains water is laid in all fields, and dustbins and skips are regularly serviced. There are electric hook-ups to numerous marked-out touring caravan pitches, and hook-ups are available for tents. We have a designated family field, and one of the most popular features of the camping site is that it is split up into numerous hedged enclosures.

We do not take advanced bookings for tents and touring caravans in the main designated area, as there is usually plenty of room, although electric hook-ups cannot be guaranteed. However we do take advanced bookings for touring caravans, only a small number of which are situated within the main caravan park. During the peak season and Bank Holidays, bookings will only be taken for a minimum of a week. Seasonal tourers are welcome, and reservations can be made for these.

Organised Camps

Organised camps for schools, scouts, guides etc are welcome, and we give quotations on enquiry. Each organised camp can have its own separate field with mains water and full facilities.

GOLDEN SUNSET HOLIDAYS
BENLLECH
ANGLESEY LL74 8SW
TEL: 01248 852345

Ratings You Can Trust

ENGLAND

The *English Tourism Council* (formerly the English Tourist Board) has joined with the *AA* and *RAC* to create a new, easily understood quality rating for serviced accommodation, giving a clear guide of what to expect.

HOTELS are given a rating from One to Five *Stars* – the more Stars, the higher the quality and the greater the range of facilities and level of services provided.

GUEST ACCOMMODATION, which includes guest houses, bed and breakfasts, inns and farmhouses, is rated from One to Five *Diamonds*. Progressively higher levels of quality and customer care must be provided for each one of the One to Five Diamond ratings.

HOLIDAY PARKS, TOURING PARKS and CAMPING PARKS are now also assessed using *Stars*. Standards of quality range from a One Star (acceptable) to a Five Star (exceptional) park.

Look out also for the new *SELF-CATERING* Star ratings. The more *Stars* (from One to Five) awarded to an establishment, the higher the levels of quality you can expect. Establishments at higher rating levels also have to meet some additional requirements for facilities.

NB Some self-catering properties had not been assessed at the time of going to press and in these cases the old-style KEY symbols will still be shown.

SCOTLAND

Star Quality Grades will reflect the most important aspects of a visit, such as the warmth of welcome, efficiency and friendliness of service, the quality of the food and the cleanliness and condition of the furnishings, fittings and decor.

THE MORE STARS, THE HIGHER THE STANDARDS.

The description, such as Hotel, Guest House, Bed and Breakfast, Lodge, Holiday Park, Self-catering etc tells you the type of property and style of operation.

WALES

Places which score highly will have an especially welcoming atmosphere and pleasing ambience, high levels of comfort and guest care, and attractive surroundings enhanced by thoughtful design and attention to detail

STAR QUALITY GUIDE FOR

HOTELS, GUEST HOUSES AND FARMHOUSES

SELF-CATERING ACCOMMODATION
(Cottages, Apartments, Houses)

CARAVAN HOLIDAY HOME PARKS
(Holiday Parks, Touring Parks, Camping Parks)

★★★★★   *Exceptional quality*
★★★★   *Excellent quality*
★★★   *Very good quality*
★★   *Good quality*
★   *Fair to good quality*

In England, Scotland and Wales, all graded properties are inspected annually by Tourist Authority trained Assessors.

Please mention Caravan & Camping when enquiring

The FHG GUIDE TO
CARAVAN AND CAMPING HOLIDAYS
2005

Many people decide to opt for a holiday 'at home' here in Britain rather than face the hassle and worry of foreign travel and, not surprisingly, caravan and camping holidays are often the first choice for those seeking an alternative. Holiday Parks may have similar facilities to those foreign holiday venues, with swimming pools, beaches nearby, entertainment, and shops and eating facilities on site. Smaller sites and touring parks also have their place, offering peace and tranquillity, variety, and the opportunity to travel the length and breadth of the country.

The FHG Guide to Caravan & Camping Holidays 2005 also offers variety. Our selection covers England, Scotland, Wales and a handful in Ireland, and includes sites for tourers, static vans and holiday parks, which often cater for the camper as well.

ENQUIRIES AND BOOKINGS Give full details of dates (with an alternative), numbers and any special requirements. Ask about any points in the holiday description which are not clear and make sure that prices and conditions are clearly explained. You should receive confirmation in writing and a receipt for any deposit or advance payment.

CANCELLATIONS A holiday booking is a form of contract with obligations on both sides. If you have to cancel, give as much notice as possible. The longer the notice the better the chance that your host can replace your booking and therefore refund any payments. If the proprietor cancels in such a way that causes serious inconvenience, he may have obligations to you which have not been properly honoured. Take advice if necessary from such organisations as the Citizen's Advice Bureau, Consumer's Association, Trading Standards Office, Local Tourist Office, etc., or your own solicitor. It is possible to ensure against cancellation – brokers and insurance companies can advise you about this.

COMPLAINTS It's best if any problems can be sorted out at the start of your holiday. You should therefore try to raise any complaints on the spot. If you do not, or if the problem is not solved, you can contact the organisations mentioned above. You can also write to us. We will follow up the complaint with the advertiser – but we cannot act as intermediaries or accept responsibility for holiday arrangements.

FHG Publications Ltd. do not inspect accommodation and an entry in our guides does not imply a recommendation. However, our advertisers have signed their agreement to work for the holidaymaker's best interests and as their customer, you have the right to expect appropriate attention and service.

For popular locations, especially during the main holiday season, you should always book in advance. Please mention *The FHG Guide to Caravan and Camping Holidays* when you are making enquiries and bookings and don't forget to use our Readers' Offer Voucher/Coupons (pages 41-68) if you're near any of the attractions which are kindly participating.

Anne Cuthbertson, *Editor*

Guide to
Caravan
& Camping
Holidays
2005

England, Scotland, Wales & Ireland
with

Caravans for Hire
Holiday Parks and Centres
Caravan Sites & Night Halts
and Camping Sites

FHG Publications, part of IPC Country & Leisure Media Ltd

FHG

Other FHG Publications

Recommended Country Hotels of Britain
Recommended Country Inns & Pubs of Britain
Recommended Short Break Holidays in Britain
Pets Welcome!
The Golf Guide: Where to Play/Where to Stay
Self-Catering Holidays in Britain
Britain's Best Holidays
Bed and Breakfast Stops
The Original Farm Holiday Guide to Coast & Country Holidays
Children Welcome! Family Holiday and Days Out Guide

ISBN 185055 369 6
© IPC Media Ltd 2005

Cover photographs:
Lakeside Caravan & Camping Site, Near Dulverton supplied by Roy J. Westlake
Cover design: Focus Network

Maps: ©MAPS IN MINUTES™ 2004. ©Crown Copyright, Ordnance Survey
Northern Ireland 2004 Permit No.NI 1675

Typeset by FHG Publications Ltd, Paisley.

Printed and bound in Great Britain by William Clowes, Beccles, Suffolk

Distribution. Book Trade: ORCA Book Services, Stanley House,
3 Fleets Lane, Poole, Dorset BH15 3AJ
(Tel: 01202 665432; Fax: 01202 666219)
e-mail: mail@orcabookservices.co.uk
News Trade: Market Force (UK) Ltd, 5th Floor Low Rise, King's Reach Tower,
Stamford Street, London SE1 9LS
Tel: 0207 633 3450; Fax: 0207 633 3572

Published by FHG Publications Ltd., Abbey Mill Business Centre,
Seedhill, Paisley PA1 ITJ (Tel: 0141-887 0428; Fax: 0141-889 7204).
e-mail: fhg@ipcmedia.com

Guide to Caravan & Camping is an FHG publication, published by
IPC Country & Leisure Media Ltd, part of IPC Media Group of Companies.

KEY TO SYMBOLS

 Caravans for Hire (one or more caravans for hire on site)

 Holiday Parks & Centres (usually larger sites hiring holiday homes/vans, with amenities)

 Caravan Sites and Night Halts (for touring caravans, caravanettes, etc)

 Camping Sites (where campers are welcome)

THE FHG DIPLOMA

HELP IMPROVE
BRITISH TOURIST STANDARDS

You are choosing holiday accommodation from our very popular FHG Publications.
Whether it be a hotel, guest house, farmhouse or self-catering accommodation, we think you will find it hospitable, comfortable and clean, and your host and hostess friendly and helpful.

Why not write and tell us about it?

As a recognition of the generally well-run and excellent holiday accommodation reviewed in our publications, we at FHG Publications Ltd. present a diploma to proprietors who receive the highest recommendation from their guests who are also readers of our Guides. If you care to write to us praising the holiday you have booked through FHG Publications Ltd. – whether this be board, self-catering accommodation, a sporting or a caravan holiday, what you say will be evaluated and the proprietors who reach our final list will be contacted.

The winning proprietor will receive an attractive framed diploma to display on his premises as recognition of a high standard of comfort, amenity and hospitality. FHG Publications Ltd. offer this diploma as a contribution towards the improvement of standards in tourist accommodation in Britain. Help your excellent host or hostess to win it!

FHG DIPLOMA

We nominate

Because

Name ....

Address..

....

Telephone No...

•• *Some Useful Guidance for Guests and Hosts* ••

Every year literally thousands of holidays, short breaks and ovemight stops are arranged through our guides, the vast majority without any problems at all. In a handful of cases, however, difficulties do arise about bookings, which often could have been prevented from the outset.

It is important to remember that when accommodation has been booked, both parties – guests and hosts – have entered into a form of contract. We hope that the following points will provide helpful guidance.

GUESTS:

• When enquiring about accommodation, be as precise as possible. Give exact dates, numbers in your party and the ages of any children.

• State the number and type of rooms wanted and also what catering you require – bed and breakfast, full board etc. Make sure that the position about evening meals is clear – and about pets, reductions for children or any other special points.

• Read our reviews carefully to ensure that the proprietors you are going to contact can supply what you want. Ask for a letter confirming all arrangements, if possible.

• If you have to cancel, do so as soon as possible. Proprietors do have the right to retain deposits and under certain circumstances to charge for cancelled holidays if adequate notice is not given and they cannot re-let the accommodation.

HOSTS:

• Give details about your facilities and about any special conditions. Explain your deposit system clearly and arrangements for cancellations, charges etc. and whether or not your terms include VAT.

• If for any reason you are unable to fulfil an agreed booking without adequate notice, you may be under an obligation to arrange suitable alternative accommodation or to make some form of compensation.

A 70-minute journey into the lost world of the English narrow gauge light railway. Features historic steam locomotives from many countries.

PETS MUST BE KEPT UNDER CONTROL AND NOT ALLOWED ON TRACKS

Open: Sundays and Bank Holiday weekends 13 March to 30 October. Additional days in summer.

Directions: on A4146 towards Hemel Hempstead, close to roundabout junction with A505.

Be a giant in a magical miniature world of make-believe depicting rural England in the 1930s. "A little piece of history that is forever England."

Open: 10am to 5pm daily mid February to end October.

Directions: Junction 16 M25, Junction 2 M40.

A working steam railway centre. Steam train rides, miniature railway rides, large collection of historic preserved steam locomotives, carriages and wagons.

Open: Sundays and Bank Holidays April to October, plus Wednesdays in June, July and August 10.30am to 5.30pm.

Directions: off A41 Aylesbury to Bicester Road, 6 miles north west of Aylesbury.

Farm animals, 18th century watermill and farmhouse, farm artifacts, caravan and camping, children's play areas. Restaurant and gift shop.

Open: all year 9.30am to 5pm.

Directions: signposted off both A47 and A1.

The unique story of the salt industry and the local history of the area. With temporary exhibitions and special events throughout the year, there is something for everyone.

Open: Tuesday to Friday (+ Mondays in August and Bank Holiday Mondays) 10am to 5pm Saturday and Sunday 2-5pm (12 noon-5pm in August)

Directions: on A533 ½ mile from town centre. Approx. 30 mins from Chester.

This delightful cornmill dates back to 1351. A guided tour of the working mill is included in the admission price.

Open: April and September weekends: 1-5pm.
May to August
Tuesday to Sunday 1-5pm
+ Bank Holiday Mondays
Directions: 10 miles from Chester, well signposted from the A534

Geevor is the largest mining history site in the UK in a spectacular setting on Cornwall's Atlantic coast. Guided underground tour, many surface buildings, museum, cafe, gift shop. Free parking.

Open: daily except Saturdays 10am to 5pm

Directions: 7 miles from Penzance beside the B3306 Land's End to St Ives coast road

A collection of cars from film and TV, including Chitty Chitty Bang Bang, James Bond's Aston Martin, Del Boy's van, Fab1 and many more.

PETS MUST BE KEPT ON LEAD

Open: daily 10am-5pm.
Closed February half term.
Weekends only in December.

Directions: in centre of Keswick close to car park.

World's finest steamboat collection and premier all-weather attraction. Swallows and Amazons exhibition, model boat pond, tea shop, souvenir shop. Free guided tours. Model boat exhibition.

Open: 10am to 5pm 3rd weekend in March to last weekend October.

Directions: on A592 half-a-mile north of Bowness-on-Windermere.

A superb family day out in the atmosphere of a bygone era. Explore the recreated period street and fascinating exhibitions. Unlimited tram rides are free with entry. Play areas, shops, tea rooms, pub, restaurant and lots more.

Open: daily April to October 10 am to 5.30pm, weekends in winter.

Directions: eight miles from M1 Junction 28, follow brown and white signs for "Tramway Museum".

FHG READERS' OFFER 2005

Blue-John Cavern

Castleton, Hope Valley, Derbyshire S33 8WP
Tel: 01433 620642 • e-mail: lesley@bluejohn.gemsoft.co.uk
website: www.bluejohn-cavern.co.uk

One child free with every paying adult

Valid until end 2005

NOT TO BE USED IN CONJUNCTION WITH ANY OTHER OFFER

FHG READERS' OFFER 2005

Treak Cliff Cavern

HOME OF BLUE JOHN STONE

Castleton, Hope Valley, Derbyshire S33 8WP
Tel: 01433 620571
e-mail: treakcliff@bluejohnstone.com • website: www.bluejohnstone.com

10% discount (not valid on Special Events days)

valid during 2005

NOT TO BE USED IN CONJUNCTION WITH ANY OTHER OFFER

FHG READERS' OFFER 2005

Crealy Adventure Park

Sidmouth Road, Clyst St Mary, Exeter, Devon EX5 1DR

Tel: 0870 116 3333• Fax: 01395 233211
website: www.crealy.co.uk

FREE superkart race or panning for gold. Height restrictions apply

valid until 31/10/05

NOT TO BE USED IN CONJUNCTION WITH ANY OTHER OFFER

FHG READERS' OFFER 2005

The Gnome Reserve & Wild Flower Garden

West Putford, Near Bradworthy, Devon EX22 7XE

Tel: 0870 845 9012 • e-mail: info@gnomereserve.co.uk
website: www.gnomereserve.co.uk

One FREE child with full paying adult

Valid during 2005

NOT TO BE USED IN CONJUNCTION WITH ANY OTHER OFFER

FHG READERS' OFFER 2005

Living Coasts

Harbourside, Beacon Quay, Torquay, Devon TQ1 2BG

Tel: 01803 202470 • Fax: 01803 202471
e-mail: info@livingcoasts.org.uk • website: www.livingcoasts.org.uk

40p OFF standard ticket price for each person

valid during 2005

NOT TO BE USED IN CONJUNCTION WITH ANY OTHER OFFER

Large range of natural water-worn caverns featuring mining equipment, stalactites and stalagmites, and fine deposits of Blue-John stone, Britain's rarest semi-precious stone.

DOGS MUST BE KEPT ON LEAD

Open: 9.30am to 5.30pm.

Directions: situated 2 miles west of Castleton; follow brown tourist signs.

FHG PUBLICATIONS, ABBEY MILL BUSINESS CENTRE, PAISLEY PA1 1TJ

An underground wonderland of stalactites, stalagmites, rocks, minerals and fossils. Home of the unique Blue John stone – see the largest single piece ever found. Suitable for all ages.

Open: opens 10am. Enquire for last tour of day and closed days.

Directions: half-a-mile west of Castleton on A6187 (old A625)

FHG PUBLICATIONS, ABBEY MILL BUSINESS CENTRE, PAISLEY PA1 1TJ

Maximum fun, magic and adventure. An unforgettable family experience, with Tidal Wave log flume, rollercoaster, Queen Bess pirate ship, techno race karts, bumper boats, Vicorian carousel, animal handling, and huge indoor and outdoor play areas. The South-West's favourite family attraction!

Open:
Summer – daily 10am to 5pm
Holiday season – daily 10am to 6pm
Winter (Nov-March) – Wed-Sun 10am-5pm

Directions: minutes from M5 Junction 30 on the A3052 Sidmouth road, near Exeter

FHG PUBLICATIONS, ABBEY MILL BUSINESS CENTRE, PAISLEY PA1 1TJ

Visit 1000+ gnomes and pixies in two-acre beech wood. Gnome hats are loaned free of charge - so the gnomes think you are one of them - don't forget your camera! Also 2-acre wild flower garden with 250 labelled species.

Open: daily 10am to 6pm 21st March to 31st October.

Directions: between Bideford and Bude; follow brown tourist signs from A39/A388/A386.

FHG PUBLICATIONS, ABBEY MILL BUSINESS CENTRE, PAISLEY PA1 1TJ

Features a range of fascinating coastal creatures from penguins to fur seals, puffins to sea ducks. Reconstructed beaches, cliff faces and an estuary. A huge meshed aviary allows birds to fly free over your head, while special tunnels give stunning crystal-clear views of the birds and seals underwater.

Open: all year from 10am to 6pm (summer) or dusk (winter)

Directions: follow brown tourist signs from Torquay. Situated right on the harbour front.

FHG PUBLICATIONS, ABBEY MILL BUSINESS CENTRE, PAISLEY PA1 1TJ

"England for Excellence" award-winning family entertainment park. Highlights: hilarious shows including the famous sheep-racing and the duck trials; the awesome Ewetopia indoor adventure playground for adults and children; brewery; mountain boarding; great local food.

Open: daily, 10am to 6pm April - Oct Phone for Winter opening times and details.

Directions: on A39 North Devon link road, two miles west of Bideford Bridge.

A picturesque 200-year old woollen mill with machinery that spins yarn and weaves cloth.
Mill machinery, restaurant, exhibition gallery, shop and gardens in a waterside setting.

Open: Museum open March to October daily 10.30am to 5pm. Mill Shop and restaurant open all year round.

Directions: Two miles from Junction 27 M5; follow signs to Willand (B3181) then brown tourist signs to Working Woollen Mill.

Voted 'Most Family-Friendly Museum 2004', Killhope is Britain's best preserved lead mining site, with lots to see and do. Underground Experience is something not to be missed.

Open: March 19th to October 31st 10.30am to 5pm daily.

Directions: alongside A689, midway between Stanhope and Alston in the heart of the North Pennines.

Craft Village with animals, museum, blacksmith, glassblowing, miniature railway (Sundays and August), craft shops, tea room and licensed restaurant.

DOGS MUST BE KEPT ON LEAD

Open: Craft Village open all year. Farm open 1st March to 31st October.

Directions: M25, A127 towards Southend. Take A176 junction off A127, 3rd exit Wash Road, 2nd left Barleylands Road.

Fantastic 'hands-on' adventure zoo farm for all ages and all weathers. 60 different species from chicks and lambs to camels and bison. New indoor and outdoor mazes (longest in world and educational). Family-friendly Cafe & Shop.

Open: from February half-term to end October 10.30am to 5pm Monday to Saturday (closed Mon + Sun in term time)

Directions: on B3128 between Bristol and Clevedon or Exit 19 or 20 from M5

On three floors of a Listed Victorian warehouse telling 200 years of inland waterway history. • Historic boats • Boat trips available (Easter to October) • Painted boat gallery • Blacksmith • Archive film • Hands-on displays "A great day out"

Open: every day 10am to 5pm (excluding Christmas Day). Last admissions 4pm

Directions: Junction 11A or 12 off M5 – follow brown signs for Historic Docks. Railway and bus station - 15 minute walk. Free coach parking.

Discover the fascinating history of cider making. There is a programme of temporary exhibitions and events plus free samples of Hereford cider brandy.

Open: April to Oct
10am to 5.30pm (daily)
Nov to Dec 11am to 3pm (daily)
Jan to Mar 11am to 3pm (Tues to Sun)
Directions: situated west of Hereford off the A438
Hereford to Brecon road.

The museum of everyday life in Roman Britain. An award-winning museum with re-created Roman rooms, hands-on discovery areas, and some of the best mosaics outside the Mediterranean.

Open: Monday to Saturday
10am-5.30pm
Sunday 2pm-5.30pm.

Directions: St Albans.

Miles of mystery and history beneath your feet! Grab a lantern and get ready for an amazing underground adventure. Your whole family can travel back in time as you explore this labyrinth of dark mysterious passageways. See the caves church, Druid altar and more. Under 16s must be accompanied by an adult.

Open: Wednesday to Sunday from 10am. Last tour 4pm. Open daily during local school holidays.

Directions: take A222 between A20 and A21; at Chislehurst railway bridge turn into station approach; turn right at end, then right again.

Kent's award-winning open air museum is home to a collection of historic buildings which house interactive exhibitions on life over the last 150 years.

Open: seven days a week from March to November.
10am to 5.30pm.

Directions: Junction 6 off M20, follow signs to Aylesford.

We are a working farm, with lots of animals to see and touch. Enjoy a walk round the Nature Trail or refreshments in the tearoom. Lots of activities during school holidays.

Open: Summer: daily 10.30am to 5pm
Winter: weekends only 10.30am to 4pm.
Directions: Junction 35 off M6, take B6254 towards Kirkby Lonsdale, then follow the brown signs.

FHG PUBLICATIONS, ABBEY MILL BUSINESS CENTRE, PAISLEY PA1 1TJ

Located in 100 acres of landscaped grounds, Snibston is a unique mixture, with historic mine buildings, outdoor science play areas, wildlife habitats and an exhibition hall housing five hands-on galleries. Cafe and gift shop.
Plus new Toy Box gallery for under 5s & 8s.

Open: seven days a week 10am to 5pm.

Directions: Junction 22 from M1, Junction 13 from M42.
Follow brown Heritage signs.

FHG PUBLICATIONS, ABBEY MILL BUSINESS CENTRE, PAISLEY PA1 1TJ

Well known for rescuing and rehabilitating orphaned and injured seal pups found washed ashore on Lincolnshire beaches. Also: penguins, aquarium, pets' corner, reptiles, Floral Palace (tropical birds and butterflies etc).

Open: daily from 10am. Closed Christmas/Boxing/New Year's Days.

Directions: at the north end of Skegness seafront.

FHG PUBLICATIONS, ABBEY MILL BUSINESS CENTRE, PAISLEY PA1 1TJ

Over 100 rides and attractions, including the Traumatizer suspended looping coaster and the Lucozade Space Shot.
New for 2004 -
Lost Dinosaurs of the Sahara

Open: March to November, times vary.
Directions: from North: M6 (Junction 31), A59, A565 from South: M6 (Junction 26), M58 (Junction 3), A570

FHG PUBLICATIONS, ABBEY MILL BUSINESS CENTRE, PAISLEY PA1 1TJ

It's time you came-n-saurus for a monster day out of discovery, adventure and fun.
Enjoy the adventure play areas, dinosaur trail, secret animal garden and lots more.

Open: Please call for specific opening times or see our website.

Directions: 9 miles from Norwich, follow the brown signs to Weston Park from the A47 or A1067

FHG PUBLICATIONS, ABBEY MILL BUSINESS CENTRE, PAISLEY PA1 1TJ

Eric St John-Foti invites you to visit his vast collections, from a Concorde engine to Barbara Cartland memorabilia and the the Magical Dickens Experience. Two amazing attractions for the price of one. Somewhere totally different, unique and interesting.

Open: 11am to 5pm (last entry 4pm) Open all year.

Directions: one mile from town centre on the A1122 Downham/Wisbech Road.

A collection of 65 aircraft and cockpit sections from across the history of aviation. Extensive aero engine and artefact displays.

Open: daily from 10am (closed Christmas period).

Directions: follow brown and white signs from A1, A46, A17 and A1133.

Travel back in time to the dark and dangerous world of intrigue and adventure of Medieval England's most endearing outlaw - Robin Hood. Story boards, exhibitions and a film show all add interest to the story.

Open: 10am -6pm, last admission 4.30pm.

Directions: follow the brown and white tourist information signs whilst heading towards the city centre.

A modern working farm with displays indoors and outdoors designed to help visitors listen, feel and learn whilst having fun. Daily baby animal holding sessions plus a large indoor play barn.

Open: daily from 10am

Directions: 12 miles from Nottingham on A614 or follow Robin Hood signs from J27 of M1.

Journey with us through 300 years of Crime and Punishment on this unique atmospheric site. Witness a real trial in the authentic Victorian courtroom. Prisoners and gaolers act as guides as you become part of history.

Open: Tuesday to Sunday 10am to 5pm peak season 10am to 4pm off-peak.

Directions: from Nottingham city centre follow the brown tourist signs.

See the steam trains from the golden age of the Great Western Railway. Steam locomotives in the original engine shed, a reconstructed country branch line, and a re-creation of Brunel's original broad gauge railway. On Steam Days there are rides in the 1930s carriages.

Open: Sat/Sun all year; daily 30 Apr to 25 Sept. 10am - 5pm weekends and Steam Days, 10am - 4pm other days and in winter.

Directions: at Didcot Parkway rail station; on A4130, signposted from M4 (Junction 13) and A34

The world's largest helicopter collection - over 70 exhibits, includes two royal helicopters, Russian Gunship and Vietnam veterans plus many award-winning exhibits. Cafe, shop. Flights.

PETS MUST BE KEPT UNDER CONTROL

Open: Wednesday to Sunday 10am to 5.30pm. Daily during school Easter and Summer holidays and Bank Holiday Mondays.
(10am to 4.30pm November to March)

Directions: Junction 21 off M5 then follow the propeller signs.

Come and meet the farm animals. Pony rides, pat-a-pet, indoor and outdoor play areas, woodland and river walks. Gift shop, tearoom. Monthly farmers' market.

DOGS MUST BE KEPT ON LEADS

Open: March to September 10.30am to 6pm

Directions: follow brown tourist signs off A12 and other roads

---

Discover 'Planet Earth' for an unforgettable experience. A unique Museum of Life, Dinosaur Safari, beautiful Water Gardens with fish and wildfowl, planthouses, themed gardens, Heritage Trail, miniature railway. Playzone includes crazy golf and adventure play area. Garden Centre and Terrace Cafe.

Open: open daily, except Christmas Day and Boxing Day.

Directions: signposted off A26 and A259.

The past is brought to life at one of the best loved family attractions in the South East. Step back in time and wander through over 30 shop and room settings.

PETS NOT ALLOWED IN CHILDREN'S PLAY AREA

Open: 9.30am to 6pm (last admission 4.45pm, one hour earlier in winter).

Directions: just off A21 in Battle High Street opposite the Abbey.

Wilderness Wood is a unique family-run working woodland in the Sussex High Weald. Explore trails and footpaths, enjoy local cakes and ices, try the adventure playground. Many special events and activities. Parties catered for.

Open: daily 10am to 5.30pm or dusk if earlier.

Directions: on the south side of the A272 in the village of Hadlow Down. Signposted with a brown tourist sign.

Europe's largest indoor family funfair, with exciting rides such as the New Rollercoaster, Disco Dodgems and Swashbuckling Pirate Ship. There's something for everyone whatever the weather!

Open: daily except Christmas Day and New Year's Day.
Mon-Sat 10am to 8pm,
Sun 11am to 6pm
(open from 12 noon Monday to Friday during term time).
Directions: signposted from the A1.

---

100 acres of parkland, home to hundreds of duck, geese, swans and flamingos. Discovery centre, cafe, gift shop; play area.

Open: every day except Christmas Day

Directions: signposted from A19, A195, A1231 and A182.

The Deep is the world's only submarium. Discover the story of the world's oceans on a dramatic journey from the beginning of time and into the future. Explore the wonders of the oceans, from the tropical lagoon to the icy waters of Antarctica, including 40 sharks and over 3000 other fish.

Open: daily 10am to 6pm
(last entry at 5pm).
Closed Christmas Eve and Christmas Day
Directions: from the North take A1/M, M62/A63. From the South take A1/M, A15/A63 follow signs to Hull city centre, then local signs to The Deep.

All types of birds of prey exhibited here, from owls and kestrels to eagles and vultures. Special flying displays 12 noon, 1.30pm and 3pm. Bird handling courses arranged for either half or full days.

Open: 10am to 4.30pm summer
10am to 4pm winter

Directions: on main A65 trunk road outside Settle.
Follow brown direction signs.

Visit James Herriot's original house recreated as it was in the 1940s. Television sets used in the series 'All Creatures Great and Small'. A new children's interactive gallery with life-size model farm animals and three rooms dedicated to the history of veterinary medicine.

Open: daily.
April to October 10am-6pm
November to March 11am to 4pm
Directions: follow signs off A1 or A19 to Thirsk, then A168, off Thirsk market place

---

The UK's first Science Adventure Centre. Explore the elements - Earth, Air, Fire and Water - and have fun firing a giant water cannon, launching rockets, exploding rock faces and working real JCBs. Two spectacular shows - The Big Melt and The Face of Steel; also new Sci Tek Playground.

Open: daily 10am to 5pm
(closed 24th-26th Dec and 1st Jan)

Directions: from M1 take Junction 33 (from south) or Junction 34 (from north), and follow signs. One mile from Meadowhall Shopping Centre

---

The Colour Museum is unique. Dedicated to the history, development and technology of colour, it is the ONLY museum of its kind in Europe. A truly colourful experience for both kids and adults, it's fun, it's informative and it's well worth a visit.

Open: Tuesday to Saturday
10am to 4pm
(last admission 3.30pm).
Directions: just off Westgate on B6144 from the city centre to Haworth.

A fascinating display of railway carriages and a wide range of railway items telling the story of rail travel over the years.

ALL PETS MUST BE KEPT ON LEADS

Open: daily 11am to 4.30pm

Directions: approximately one mile from Keighley on A629 Halifax road. Follow brown tourist signs

---

Visitor Centre dedicated to the much-loved Scottish writer Lewis Grassic Gibbon. Exhibition, cafe, gift shop. Outdoor children's play area. Disabled access throughout.

Open: daily April to October 10am to 4.30pm. Groups by appointment including evenings.

Directions: on the B967, accessible and signposted from both A90 and A92.

FHG
READERS'
OFFER
2005

Oban Rare Breeds Farm Park
Glencruitten, Oban, Argyll PA34 4QB
Tel: 01631 770608
e-mail: info@obanrarebreeds.com • website: www.obanrarebreeds.com

20% DISCOUNT on all admissions

valid during 2005

FHG
READERS'
OFFER
2005

Inveraray Jail
Church Square, Inveraray, Argyll PA32 8TX
Tel: 01499 302381• Fax: 01499 302195
e-mail: inverarayjail@btclick.com • website: www.inverarayjail.co.uk

one child FREE with one full-paying adult

valid until end 2005

FHG
READERS'
OFFER
2005

Kelburn Castle & Country Centre
Fairlie, Near Largs, Ayrshire KA29 0BE
Tel: 01475 568685 • e-mail: admin@kelburncountrycentre.com
website: www.kelburncountrycentre.com

One child FREE for each full paying adult

Valid until October 2005

FHG
READERS'
OFFER
2005

Scottish Maritime Museum
Harbourside, Irvine, Ayrshire KA12 8QE
Tel: 01294 278283 • e-mail: smm@tildesley.fsbusiness.co.uk
website: www.scottishmaritimemuseum.org • Fax: 01294 313211

TWO for the price of ONE

Valid from January to December 2005

FHG
READERS'
OFFER
2005

MYRETON MOTOR MUSEUM
Aberlady, East Lothian EH32 0PZ
Tel: 01875 870288

One child FREE with each paying adult

valid during 2005

Rare breeds of farm animals, pets' corner, conservation groups, tea room, woodland walk in beautiful location

Open: 10am to 6pm
mid-March to end October

Directions: two-and-a-half miles from Oban along Glencruitten road

---

19th century prison with fully restored 1820 courtroom and two prisons. Guides in uniform as warders, prisoners and matron. Remember your camera!

Open:
April to October 9.30am - 6pm
(last admission 5pm)
November to March 10am - 5pm
(last admission 4pm)
Directions: A83 to Campbeltown

The historic home of the Earls of Glasgow. Waterfalls, gardens, famous Glen, unusual trees. Riding school, stockade, play areas, exhibitions, shop, cafe and The Secret Forest. Falconry Centre.
PETS MUST BE KEPT ON LEAD

Open: daily 10am to 6pm
Easter to October.

Directions: on A78 between Largs and Fairlie,
45 minutes' drive from Glasgow.

Scotland's seafaring heritage is among the world's richest and you can relive the heyday of Scottish shipping at the Maritime Museum.

Open: all year except Christmas and New Year Holidays.
10am - 5pm
Directions: Situated on Irvine harbourside and only a 10 minute walk from Irvine train station.

On show is a large collection, from 1899, of cars, bicycles, motor cycles and commercials. There is also a large collection of period advertising, posters and enamel signs.

Open: daily April to October
11am to 4pm
November to March:
weekends 11am to 3pm or
by special appointment.

Directions: off A198 near Aberlady.
Two miles from A1.

FHG
**READERS'
OFFER
2005**

Scottish Seabird Centre

The Harbour, North Berwick, East Lothian EH39 4SS

Tel: 01620 890202 • Fax: 01620 890222

e-mail: info@seabird.org • website: www.seabird.org

any TWO admissions for the price of ONE

valid until
1st October 2005

FHG
**READERS'
OFFER
2005**

Edinburgh Butterfly & Insect World

Dobbies Garden World, Melville Nursery, Lasswade EH18 1AZ

Tel: 0131-663 4932 • Fax: 0131 654 2774

info@edinburgh-butterfly-world.co.uk • www.edinburgh-butterfly-world.co.uk

one child FREE with each full-paying adult

valid from 1st Jan 2005
to 30th April 2005

FHG
**READERS'
OFFER
2005**

The Scottish Mining Museum

Lady Victoria Colliery, Newtongrange, Midlothian EH22 4QN

Tel: 0131-663 7519 • Fax: 0131-654 0952

visitorservices@scottishminingmuseum.com • www.scottishminingmuseum.com

one child FREE with full-paying adult

valid January to
December 2005

FHG
**READERS'
OFFER
2005**

Scottish Deer Centre

Cupar, Fife KY15 4NQ

Tel: 01337 810391 • Fax: 01337 810477

TWO for ONE

valid from 1st Jan 2005
to 31st Dec 2005

FHG
**READERS'
OFFER
2005**

the scottish fisheries museum

Harbourhead, Anstruther, Fife KY10 3AB

Tel: 01333 310628

e-mail: info@scottish-fisheries-museum.org

Accompanied children FREE - maximum 5 per party

valid until end 2005

Get close to Nature with a visit to this stunning award-winning Centre. With panoramic views across the islands of the Firth of Forth and the sandy beaches of North Berwick, the area is a haven for wildlife. Live 'Big Brother' cameras zoom in really close to see a variety of wildlife including gannets, puffins, seals and sometimes even dolphins. Wildlife boat safaris and passenger ferry to Fife in summer.

Open: daily from 10am

Directions: from A1 take road for North Berwick; near the harbour; Centre signposted.

It's Creeping, It's Crawling, It's a Jungle in there! Free-flying exotic butterflies, roaming iguanas, giant pythons, 'glow in the dark' scorpions, and 'Bugs and Beasties' handling and phobia-curing sessions. Incredible leaf-cutting ants.

Open: summer 9.30am to 5.30pm winter 10am to 5pm

Directions: just off Edinburgh City Bypass at Gilmerton exit or Sheriffhall Roundabout

---

visitscotland 5-Star Attraction with two floors of interactive exhibitions and a 'Magic Helmet' tour of the pithead, re-created coal road and coal face. Largest working winding engine in Britain.

Open: daily. Summer: 10am to 5pm (last tour 3.30pm). Winter: 10am to 4pm (last tour 2.30pm)

Directions: 5 minutes from Sherrifhall Roundabout on Edinburgh City Bypass on A7 south

---

8 species of deer from around the world. Birds of prey flying demonstrations, indoor and outdoor play areas. Visit our Wolfwood. Courtyard shopping and coffee shop.

Open: daily except Christmas and New Year's Day. Summer 10am to 5pm Winter 10am to 4pm

Directions: on the A91 just 12 miles from St Andrews

In the heart of the Fife fishing community, the Museum tells and researches the story of the Scottish fishing industry and its people from the earliest times to the present. The comprehensive collection includes ships, models, paintings, photographs, equipment and the written word.

Open: daily. Apr-Sept 10am to 5.30pm (4.30pm Sun); Oct-Mar 10am to 4pm (12 to 4pm Sun)

Directions: on coast road, 10 miles south of St Andrews

FHG READERS' OFFER 2005

Landmark Forest Theme Park

Carrbridge, Inverness-shire PH23 3AJ

Tel: 01479 841613 • Freephone 0800 731 3446

e-mail: landmarkcentre@btconnect.com • website: www.landmark-centre.co.uk

10% DISCOUNT for pet owners. Free admission for pets!
Maximum of four persons per voucher

Valid during 2005

NOT TO BE USED IN CONJUNCTION WITH ANY OTHER OFFER

FHG READERS' OFFER 2005

Highland and Rare Breeds Farm

Elphin, Near Ullapool, Sutherland IV27 4HH

Tel: 01854 666204

One FREE adult or child with adult paying full entrance price

valid May to September 2005

NOT TO BE USED IN CONJUNCTION WITH ANY OTHER OFFER

FHG READERS' OFFER 2005

Speyside Heather Garden & Visitor Centre

Speyside Heather Centre, Dulnain Bridge, Inverness-shire PH26 3PA

Tel: 01479 851359 • Fax: 01479 851396

e-mail: enquiries@heathercentre.com • website: www.heathercentre.com

FREE entry to 'Heather Story' exhibition

valid during 2005

NOT TO BE USED IN CONJUNCTION WITH ANY OTHER OFFER

FHG READERS' OFFER 2005

New Lanark World Heritage Site

New Lanark Mills, New Lanark, Lanarkshire ML11 9DB

Tel: 01555 661345• Fax: 01555 665738

e-mail: visit@newlanark.org • website: www.newlanark.org

One FREE child with every full price adult

valid until 31st October 2005

NOT TO BE USED IN CONJUNCTION WITH ANY OTHER OFFER

FHG READERS' OFFER 2005

Finlaystone Country Estate

Langbank, Renfrewshire PA14 6TJ

Tel & Fax: 01475 540505

e-mail: info@finlaystone.co.uk • website: www.finlaystone.co.uk

TWO for the price of ONE

valid until April 2005

NOT TO BE USED IN CONJUNCTION WITH ANY OTHER OFFER

Great day out for all the family.
Wild Water Coaster*, Microworld
exhibition, Forest Trails, Viewing Tower,
Climbing Wall*, Tree Top Trail, Steam
powered Sawmill*, Clydesdale Horse*.
Shop, restaurant and snackbar.
(* Easter to October)
DOGS MUST BE KEPT ON LEADS

Open: daily (except Christmas Day
and attractions marked*).

Directions: 23 miles south
of Inverness at Carrbridge,
just off the A9.

FHG PUBLICATIONS, ABBEY MILL BUSINESS CENTRE, PAISLEY PA1 1TJ

Highland croft open to visitors for
"hands-on" experience with over
30 different breeds of farm animals
"stroke the goats and scratch the
pigs". Farm information centre and
old farm implements.
For all ages, cloud or shine!

Open: July and August 10am to 5pm.

Directions: On A835
15 miles north of Ullapool

FHG PUBLICATIONS, ABBEY MILL BUSINESS CENTRE, PAISLEY PA1 1TJ

Award-winning attraction with
unique 'Heather Story' exhibition,
gallery, giftshop, large garden
centre selling 300 different
heathers, antique shop, children's
play area and famous
Clootie Dumpling restaurant.

Open: all year except Christmas Day.

Directions: just off A95 between
Aviemore and Grantown-on-Spey.

FHG PUBLICATIONS, ABBEY MILL BUSINESS CENTRE, PAISLEY PA1 1TJ

A beautifully restored cotton mill
village close to the Falls of Clyde.
Explore the fascinating history of the
village, try the 'New Millennium
Experience', a magical ride which
takes you back in time to discover
what life used to be like.

Open: 11am to 5pm daily.
Closed Christmas Day
and New Year's Day.

Directions: 25 miles from Glasgow
and 35 miles from Edinburgh;
well signposted on all major routes.

FHG PUBLICATIONS, ABBEY MILL BUSINESS CENTRE, PAISLEY PA1 1TJ

Colourful gardens, imaginative
woodland play areas and tumbling
waterfalls. The Estate combines
history with adventure in a fun day
out for all the family, where your
dog can run freely. Step back in
time and uncover its secrets.

Open:
daily 10.30am to 5pm

Directions: off A8 west of Langbank,
20 minutes west of Glasgow Airport.

FHG PUBLICATIONS, ABBEY MILL BUSINESS CENTRE, PAISLEY PA1 1TJ

FHG MUSEUM OF CHILDHOOD MEMORIES

READERS' OFFER 2005

1 Castle Street, Beaumaris, Anglesey LL58 8AP

Tel: 01248 712498

website: www.aboutbritain.com/museumofchildhoodmemories.htm

One child FREE with two adults

valid during 2005

NOT TO BE USED IN CONJUNCTION WITH ANY OTHER OFFER

FHG Llanberis Lake Railway

READERS' OFFER 2005

Gilfach Ddu, Llanberis, Gwynedd LL55 4TY

Tel: 01286 870549 • e-mail: info@lake-railway.co.uk
website: www.lake-railway.co.uk

One pet travels FREE with each full fare paying adult

Valid Easter to October 2005

NOT TO BE USED IN CONJUNCTION WITH ANY OTHER OFFER

FHG Alice in Wonderland Centre

READERS' OFFER 2005

3/4 Trinity Square, Llandudno, Conwy, North Wales LL30 2PY

Tel: 01492 860082 • e-mail: alice@wonderland.co.uk
website: www.wonderland.co.uk

One child FREE with two paying adults. Guide Dogs welcome

valid during 2005

NOT TO BE USED IN CONJUNCTION WITH ANY OTHER OFFER

FHG Felinwynt RAINFOREST & BUTTERFLY CENTRE

READERS' OFFER 2005

Felinwynt, Cardigan, Ceredigion SA43 1RT

Tel: 01239 810882

website: www.butterflycentre.co.uk

TWO for the price of ONE (one voucher per party only)

valid until end October 2005

NOT TO BE USED IN CONJUNCTION WITH ANY OTHER OFFER

FHG Rhondda Heritage Park

READERS' OFFER 2005

Lewis Merthyr Colliery, Coed Cae Road, Trehafod, Near Pontypridd CF37 7NP

Tel: 01443 682036 • e-mail: info@rhonddaheritagepark.com
website: www.rhonddaheritagepark.com

Two adults or children for the price of one when accompanied by a full paying adult

Valid until end 2005 for full tours only. Not valid on special event days.

NOT TO BE USED IN CONJUNCTION WITH ANY OTHER OFFER

*Nine rooms in a Georgian house
filled with items illustrating
the happier times of family life
over the past 150 years.
Joyful nostalgia unlimited.*

Open:
March to end October

Directions:
opposite Beaumaris Castle

FHG PUBLICATIONS, ABBEY MILL BUSINESS CENTRE, PAISLEY PA1 1TJ

---

*A 60-minute ride along the shores
of beautiful Padarn Lake behind a
quaint historic steam engine.
Magnificent views of the mountains
from lakeside picnic spots.*

**DOGS MUST BE KEPT ON LEAD AT ALL TIMES
ON TRAIN**

Open: most days Easter to October.
Free timetable leaflet on request.

Directions: just off A4086 Caernarfon
to Capel Curig road at Llanberis;
follow 'Country Park' signs.

FHG PUBLICATIONS, ABBEY MILL BUSINESS CENTRE, PAISLEY PA1 1TJ

---

*Walk through the Rabbit Hole to
the colourful scenes of
Lewis Carroll's classic story set in
beautiful life-size displays.
Recorded commentaries and
transcripts available in
several languages.*

Open: all year 10am to 5pm but
closed Sundays in winter and
Christmas/Boxing Day/New Year's Day.

Directions: situated just off
the main street, 250 yards
from coach and rail stations.

FHG PUBLICATIONS, ABBEY MILL BUSINESS CENTRE, PAISLEY PA1 1TJ

---

*Mini-rainforest full of tropical plants
and exotic butterflies. Personal
attention of the owner, Mr John
Devereux. Gift shop, cafe, video room,
exhibition. Suitable for disabled visitors.
WTB Quality Assured Visitor Attraction.*

PETS NOT ALLOWED IN TROPICAL HOUSE ONLY

Open: daily Easter to end October
10.30am to 5pm

Directions: 7 miles north of Cardigan
on Aberystwyth road.
Follow brown tourist signs on A487.

FHG PUBLICATIONS, ABBEY MILL BUSINESS CENTRE, PAISLEY PA1 1TJ

---

*Make a pit stop whatever the weather!
Join an ex-miner on a tour of discovery,
ride the cage to pit bottom and take a
thrilling ride back to the surface.
Multi-media presentations, period
village street, children's adventure
play area, restaurant and gift shop.
Disabled access with assistance.*

Open: Open daily 10am to 6pm (last tour
4.30pm). Closed Mondays October to
Easter, also Dec 25th to 3rd Jan inclusive.

Directions: Exit Junction 32 M4, signposted
from A470 Pontypridd. Trehafod is located
between Pontypridd and Porth.

FHG PUBLICATIONS, ABBEY MILL BUSINESS CENTRE, PAISLEY PA1 1TJ

Berkshire

CARAVAN SITES AND NIGHT HALTS

MAIDENHEAD

⊞ ⑤ Å

See also Colour Display Advertisement

Hurley Riverside Park, Hurley, Maidenhead SL6 5NE (01628 823501/824493). Family-run park situated in the picturesque Thames Valley alongside the Thames Path. Ideal location for visiting Windsor, Legoland, Oxford and London. Multiservice and electric hook-ups. Tourers, tents and motorhomes welcome. Shop, toilet blocks with all main services, disabled facilities. Slipway, riverside walks, fishing in season. Open 1st March – 31st October. Brochure on request. **ETC ★★★★,** *DAVID BELLAMY GOLD AWARD.*
e-mail: info@hurleyriversidepark.co.uk
website: www.hurleyriversidepark.co.uk

WOKINGHAM

⑤ Å

See also Colour Display Advertisement

California Chalet & Touring Park, Nine Mile Ride, Finchampstead, Wokingham RG40 4HU (0118 973 3928; Fax: 0118 932 8720). Small, family-run park alongside a lake. Secluded pitches in a wooded setting. Close to London, Windsor and Oxford. Also available, 10 self-catering holiday chalets. Terms on request. **ETC ★★★★, AA** *THREE PENNANTS.*

A useful Index of Towns/Villages and Counties appears on page 174 – please also refer to Contents Page 3.

Buckinghamshire

CARAVAN SITES AND NIGHT HALTS

BEACONSFIELD

Mr M.J. Penfold, Highclere Farm, New Barn Lane, Seer Green, Near Beaconsfield HP9 2QZ (Tel & Fax: 01494 874505). Quiet, level meadowland park. Ideal for touring London, train station one mile. 25 minutes to Marylebone, cheap day return fares available. Legoland 12 miles, with Windsor Castle and the Thames. Model village three miles, many local attractions, including rare breeds farm. Local inn for food quarter of a mile. Lots of walks, ideal for dogs. Bed and Breakfast accommodation also available. New £100,000 shower block for 2004, new tenting area. 65 pitches available. Tourers from £12 to £16, tents from £10 to £16, motor homes £12 to £16, electric point £2. Open March to January. **ETC ★★★★** *TOURING PARK*, **AA** *THREE PENNANTS*.
e-mail: highclerepark@aol.com
website: www.highclerefarmpark.co.uk

Cheshire

CARAVAN SITES AND NIGHT HALTS

HOLMES CHAPEL (near)

Woodlands Park, Wash Lane, Allostock WA16 9LG (01565 723429 or 01332 810818). Woodlands Park is a 16-acre residential and holiday home park set in delightful shrubbery and mature woodland. The park offers homes for sale and has a flat, spacious area for tourers and tents. Facilities include toilet block with showers, laundry room, chemical toilet disposal, electric hook-up points and some hard standings. Pets welcome by arrangement. Open 1st March to 7th January. Brochure and tariff available upon request.

WARRINGTON

Hollybank Caravan Park, Warburton Bridge Road, Rixton, Warrington WA3 6HU (0161-775 2842). Quiet park in picturesque rural setting. 75 touring pitches, electric hook-ups, modern toilet blocks, showers and hot water (free), central heating, shop, phone and launderette, Calor and Gaz, games room. Ideal base for touring North West, Peak District, Yorkshire Dales and a convenient night halt off M6, M56, M60. Open all year. Brochure available. Directions: two miles east off Junction 21 M6 on A57 (Irlam). Turn right at lights into Warburton Bridge Road; entry on left. **ETC ★★★★**, **AA** *THREE PENNANTS*

Cornwall

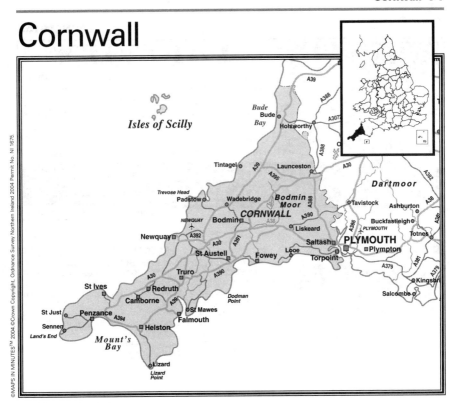

CARAVANS FOR HIRE

☀ 🚐 🅿 👤

HELSTON (near)

Boscrege Caravan & Camping Park, Ashton, Near Helston TR13 9TG (01736 762231). Nestling amongst a myriad of wild flower-lined Cornish lanes, but still with easy access in a designated Area of Outstanding Natural Beauty, secret, hidden Boscrege offers luxury caravans and camping in this haven of tranquillity. It is centrally situated for exploring West Cornwall, a land famous for its myths and legends as well as its rugged beauty, coves and fishing villages. The park has been extensively landscaped and refurbished and specialises in holidays for families and couples. Special out of season offers. Free showers. Games room. Children play area. Pets welcome.

e-mail: enquiries@caravanparkcornwall.com
website: www.caravanparkcornwall.com

©MAPS IN MINUTES™ 2004 ©Crown Copyright. Ordnance Survey Northern Ireland 2004 Permit No. NI 1675.

LOOE

See also Colour Display Advertisement

Mr P. Hannay, Tregoad Park, St Martins, Looe PL13 1PB (01503 262718; Fax: 01503 264777). Close to Looe, a quality family touring site with south-facing pitches and fantastic views to the sea. Outdoor heated pool, children's splash pool, children's adventure area, widescreen cinema, crazy golf, family bathrooms and games area. Also laundry; free showers; electric hook-ups; licensed bar/bistro; shop. Modern statics available. Bed and Breakfast. Rally enquiries welcome.
e-mail: info@tregoadpark.co.uk
website: www.tregoadpark.co.uk

MAWGAN PORTH

See also Colour Display Advertisement

Marver Holiday Park, Mawgan Porth, Near Newquay TR8 4BB (Tel & Fax: 01637 860493). Small, quiet family-run site. Offering beautiful views of the Lanherne valley. Approximately 150 yards from the beach, which is excellent for children, surfers and fishing. Only five miles from Newquay and eight miles from the historic fishing port of Padstow. The site offers chalets and static caravans for hire and a level campsite suitable for caravans, motor homes and tents. On site there is a toilet and shower block, sauna and launderette, in which there is a payphone, washing up facilities and a freezer for the use of our guests. Nearby fishing, surfing, horse riding, golf and shops, also good public houses, surf board and wet suit hire.
e-mail: familyholidays@aol.com

NEWQUAY

Quarryfield Caravan & Camping Park, Crantock, Newquay. Superbly situated in Cornwall, overlooking beautiful Crantock Bay and the sheltered waters of the River Gannel Estuary. Quarryfield is the ideal spot for the freedom of a self-catering, caravan and camping holiday. Caravans accommodating up to eight people are available for hire, early booking recommended. All fully equipped, except towels and bed linen. Separate, level well drained field for tents with plenty of space. Campers and tourers are welcome to use the bar, pool and Children's Playing Area. Facilities include - licensed bar, heated swimming pool, games room, self-service shop, modern toilet facilities, laundry room with large sinks, iron, spin/tumble drier. There is also ample parking alongside each caravan or tent. Owned and managed by the same family since 1938. **Contact: Mrs Winn, Tretherras, Newquay TR7 2RE (01637 872792).**

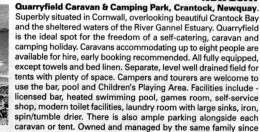

PADSTOW

Mrs M.J. Raymont, Trevean Farm, St Merryn, Padstow PL28 8PR (01841 520772). Small, pleasant site close to several sandy beaches with good surfing and lovely, golden sands. Rural area with splendid sea views. Riding school and golf club within two miles. Village shops one mile. Sea and river fishing nearby. Padstow and Camel Estuary four miles. Three static six-berth luxury caravans with cooker, fridge, mains water supply, flush toilet, shower and colour TV. Good approach from B road. Tourers and campers welcome. Modern toilet/shower block with free showers. Electric hook-ups. Pay phone, children's play area and small shop (Whitsun to September) on-site. Pets permitted in tents and tourers but not in static caravans. Weekly rates for static vans from £150 to £375 according to season.
Touring caravans and tents from £8 to £10 per night. Open Easter to October. **ETC ★★★**

PENZANCE

C. Hichens, Carne Cottage, Morvah, Pendeen, Penzance TR19 7TT (01736 788309; mobile: 07733 486347). Carne Farm is a working dairy farm situated on the North Cornish Coast, one mile from the nearest beach at Portherras Cove. It is excellent for walking, close to coastal footpath and with climbing nearby. Visitors are only six miles from Penzance, eight miles from St Ives and two miles from the nearest village shop, pubs and restaurants at Pendeen. The spacious eight- berth caravan is located in the field above the farmhouse, with fenced lawn and garden furniture, and has lovely views of fields, moorland and sea. It has a double bedroom, twin bedroom/cot, shower and toilet. It is equipped with electricity, fridge, full sized cooker, fire and hot and cold water, duvets, pillows and kitchen equipment. Television. Linen provided. Visitors welcome on the farm. Babysitting available. Rates from £120 to £220. Basic Camping available. Ring for details.

PENZANCE

Roselands Caravan & Camping Park, Dowran, St Just, Penzance TR19 7RS (01736 788571). A quiet, secluded, small, family-run park in the middle of nowhere, but close to everywhere. Luxury caravans. Level touring pitches. Bar. Breakfast and Evening Meals in our new conservatory. Games room and play area. Shop and launderette. **ETC ★★★, AA** *THREE PENNANTS*
e-mail: **camping@roseland84.freeserve.co.uk**
website: **www.roselands.co.uk**

WADEBRIDGE

Mrs E Hodge, Pengelly Farm, Burlawn, Wadebridge PL27 7LA (01208 814217). One only, 2004 luxury, fully serviced and equipped, self-contained, two-bedroomed static caravan in quiet location on working dairy farm overlooking wooded valleys. Large garden with patio table and chairs plus own barbecue. An ideal location for a touring, walking and cycling base. Only six miles from the coast, with sailing, surfing, golf, riding and coastal walks. Camel Trail, Saints Way and Pencarrow House nearby. The Eden Project 35 minutes' drive, Padstow 20 minutes. Wadebridge one-and-a-half miles with shopping, pubs, restaurants and leisure facilities. Farmhouse B&B also available. **ETC** *INSPECTED.*
e-mail: **hodgepete@hotmail.com**
website: **www.pengellyfarm.co.uk**

HOLIDAY PARKS AND CENTRES

BUDE

Wooda Farm Park. A real Cornish welcome awaits you from the Colwill family. Enjoy a farm and seaside holiday with us. We offer luxury holiday homes and excellent facilities for touring and camping. Shop and laundry room. Activities include playground, coarse fishing, short golf course. In main season; indoor archery, tractor and trailor rides and clay pigeon shooting. Down at the farm there is a restaurant take-away and beer garden. Also farmyard friends. Sandy beaches one and-a-quarter miles. Splash indoor pool nearby. Local village inn five minutes walk. Write, phone or fax for brochure and tariff to: **Mrs G. Colwill, Wooda Farm Park, Poughill, Bude EX23 9HJ (01288 352 069; Fax: 01288 355 258). ETC ★★★★★ AA** *FIVE PENNANTS PREMIER PARK, THE BEST OF BRITISH TOURING & HOLIDAY PARKS.*

DAVID BELLAMY GOLD CONSERVATION AWARD,
e-mail: enquiries@wooda.co.uk   **website: www.wooda.co.uk**

BUDE (near)
See also Colour Display Advertisement

Widemouth Bay Caravan Park. Overlooking beautiful Widemouth Bay, our 50-acre Park is only a few minutes from a safe, sandy beach. New tropical indoor heated pool. Children's club, safe playground. Electric hook-ups, launderette, shop/ takeaway, club. Free hot showers, free awning space, free entertainment, free licensed club. All enquiries to: **Dept. AA, John Fowler Holidays, Marlborough Road, Ilfracombe EX34 8PF (Booking Hotline: 01271 866766).**
website: www.johnfowlerholidays.com

HELSTON
See also Colour Display Advertisement

Sea Acres Holiday Park, Helston (01326 290064). Nestling on the stunning Lizard Peninsula with breathtaking views overlooking Kennack Sands Beach. Indoor heated swimming pool and family entertainment. For a free colour brochure or to make a booking call **Parkdean Holidays** on **0870 420 5607.**
ETC ★★★★
e-mail: enquiries@parkdeanholidays.co.uk
website: www.parkdeanholidays.co.uk

☼ 🏕 ⚐

NEWQUAY
See also Colour Display Advertisement

Trevarrian Holiday Park, Mawgan Porth, Newquay TR8 4AG (01637 860381). Situated in quiet countryside close to fabulous beaches. Superb facilities include heated pool, self-service shop, launderette, TV/video and games room, children's play area, tennis court and pitch and putt. Free evening entertainment during peak season. "Stimbles" with club licence, bar snacks. Individual pitches, electric hook-ups available, modern toilets and hot showers. No overcrowding. Park lighting. Write or phone for free colour brochure. **AA** *FOUR PENNANTS*.
e-mail: holidays@trevarrian.co.uk
website: www.trevarrian.co.uk

🚐 ☼ 🏕 ⚐

NEWQUAY
See also Colour Display Advertisement

Newquay Holiday Park, Newquay (01637 871111). The on-park facilities and superb countryside location mean Newquay is one of the best family holiday centres in Cornwall. Eleven beaches and a bustling town centre nearby, outdoor heated pools, kids' clubs and family entertainment. For a free colour brochure or to make a booking call **Parkdean Holidays** on **0870 420 5607.** ETC ★★★★, **AA** *HOLIDAY CENTRE.*
e-mail: enquiries@parkdeanholidays.co.uk
website: www.parkdeanholidays.co.uk

🚐 ☼ 🏕 ⚐

NEWQUAY
See also Colour Display Advertisement

Holywell Bay Holiday Park, Newquay (01637 871111). Holywell enjoys a lovely, peaceful setting, nestling in a narrow valley on the Cornish coastline, opening up to the fantastic Holywell beach. Outdoor heated pool with slide, family entertainment and kids' club. For a free colour brochure or to make a booking call **Parkdean Holidays** on **0870 420 5607.** ETC ★★★★, **AA** *HOLIDAY CENTRE.*
e-mail: enquiries@parkdeanholidays.co.uk
website: www.parkdeanholidays.co.uk

🚐 ☼ 🏕 ⚐

NEWQUAY
See also Colour Display Advertisement

White Acres Country Park, White Cross, Newquay (01726 862100). 5 star award-winning park set in 170 acres of superb countryside with magnificent fishing lakes. Only a few miles from Newquay's glorious beaches. The park is packed with facilities for families and anglers. Indoor heated pool, live entertainment and superb kids' clubs. For a free colour brochure or to make a booking call **Parkdean Holidays** on **0870 420 5607.** ETC ★★★★★, **AA** *HOLIDAY CENTRE, ROSE AWARD.*
e-mail: enquiries@parkdeanholidays.co.uk
website: www.whiteacres.co.uk

NEWQUAY (near)
See also Colour Display Advertisement

Crantock Bay Holiday Park, near Newquay (01637 831005). Boasting an enviable location with views across the beach and river estuary. Light entertainment, bar and patio area. For a free colour brochure or to make a booking call **Parkdean Holidays** on **0870 420 5607**. ETC ★★★★
e-mail: enquiries@parkdeanholidays.co.uk
website: www.parkdeanholidays.co.uk

REDRUTH

Mr & Mrs J Rielly, Lanyon Caravan and Camping Park, Four Lanes, Redruth TR16 6LP (01209 313474; Fax: 01209 313422). For those wanting a memorable holiday look no further. We have lots to offer you. Superb central location surrounded by beautiful countryside. A range of caravans to suit all pockets. Indoor heated pool. All day games room. Bar/Restaurant/Takeaway/Free entertainment in high season. Two play areas. Upgraded toilet/bath/shower block. Launderette/dish washing facility/free hot water. Spacious level pitches and short grass. Best of all, you will be looked after by caring residential family. ETC ★★★★, AA *THREE PENNANTS*.
website: www.lanyonholidaypark.co.uk
or   www.lanyoncaravanandcampingpark.co.uk

REDRUTH

Tehidy Holiday Park, Harris Mill, Illogan, Redruth TR16 4JQ (01209 216489). Small family-run park in a peaceful wooded location, ideally situated to explore the rugged beauty of the north coast's magnificent beaches, and southern coast line. We are a short distance to local amenities including surfing, sailing, fishing, golf, riding and leisure centre. Redruth approximately two miles, Portreath approximately two miles. One, two and three bedroom caravans, two bedroom bungalows. Two wheelchair-friendly; clean, comfortable and reasonably priced including VAT, gas, electricity and colour TV. Tent and touring pitches with electric hook-up, toilet block with showers. Children's play area, shop/off-licence, launderette, games room, pay phone. Send or telephone for brochure.
website: www.tehidy.co.uk

ST AGNES
See also Colour Display Advertisement

Chiverton Park, Blackwater, Truro TR4 8HS (01872 560667). Set in the heart of glorious Cornish countryside, yet only a short distance from the A30, this spacious, well-run park offers peace and relaxation in a delightful four-acre rural setting. Caravan holiday homes - touring and camping. North coast three miles, Truro five. Families and couples; pets welcome. Peace and quiet - no club or bar. Shop/off licence, laundry room, games room, children's play area. Electric hook-ups. Satellite TV in all units. Holiday homes are fully equipped (except linen, which may be hired).
e-mail: info@chivertonpark.co.uk
website: www.chivertonpark.co.uk

▱ ☼ 🅢 Å | See also Colour Display Advertisement

St Minver Holiday Park, Wadebridge (01208 862305). A spacious and attractive park surrounded by rolling Cornish countryside, only a few miles from Rock and Polzeath beaches. Indoor heated pool, kids' club and live family entertainment. For a free colour brochure or to make a booking call **Parkdean Holidays** on **0870 420 5607. ETC ★★★★, AA** *HOLIDAY CENTRE, ROSE AWARD.*
e-mail: **enquiries@parkdeanholidays.co.uk**
website: **www.parkdeanholidays.co.uk**

CARAVAN SITES AND NIGHT HALTS

BUDE

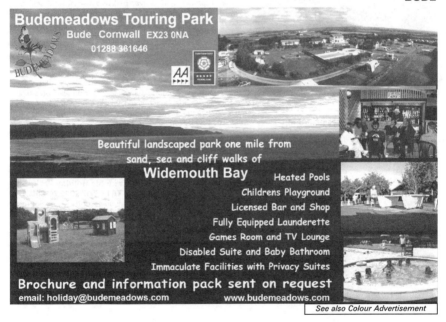

Budemeadows Touring Park
Bude Cornwall EX23 0NA
01288 361646

AA ★★★★★ ▶▶▶▶

Beautiful landscaped park one mile from sand, sea and cliff walks of
Widemouth Bay
Heated Pools
Childrens Playground
Licensed Bar and Shop
Fully Equipped Launderette
Games Room and TV Lounge
Disabled Suite and Baby Bathroom
Immaculate Facilities with Privacy Suites
Brochure and information pack sent on request
email: holiday@budemeadows.com   www.budemeadows.com

See also Colour Advertisement

▱ 🅢 Å | **BUDE**

Cornish Coasts Caravan & Camping Park, Middle Penlean, Poundstock, Widemouth Bay, Bude EX23 0EE (01288 361380). Our site is a peaceful, friendly site with glorious views over countryside and coastline. Only two miles from the sandy and surfing beach of Widemouth Bay. An ideal base for touring Devon and Cornwall, also walking the spectacular North Cornwall Coastal Path (walking groups welcomed). Toilets, showers, dishwashing area, laundry, electric hook-ups, children's play area, shop, level touring/tent pitches with easy access from £6 to £9. Four two/six berth holiday caravans to let. Please phone or write for brochure. **AA** *THREE PENNANTS. BATB (BUDE AREA TOURIST BOARD). CORNWALL TOURIST BOARD REGISTERED ACCOMMODATION.*

e-mail: **reception4@cornishcoasts.co.uk**   website: **www.cornishcoasts.co.uk**

BUDE

Upper Lynstone Caravan and Camping Park, Bude EX23 0LP (01288 352017: Fax: 01288 359034). Upper Lynstone is a family-run park situated just three-quarters of a mile from Bude's town centre on the coastal road to Widemouth Bay. Bude's shops, beaches with outdoor pool, bars and restaurants are all within walking distance. Enjoy the breathtaking beauty of the Cornish Coast from the footpath that leads from our park. The park has modern caravans for hire and spacious camping and touring fields with electric hook-ups. Facilities include a small but well equipped shop, free showers, laundry room, telephone and children's play area. We are also Calor and Camping Gas stockists. Well-behaved dogs welcome. **ETC ★★★★, AA** *THREE PENNANTS.*
e-mail: reception@upperlynstone.co.uk
website: www.upperlynstone.co.uk

CRACKINGTON HAVEN

Hentervene Caravan and Camping Park, Crackington Haven, Near Bude EX23 0LF (01840 230365). Peaceful family-run camping and caravan park two miles from Crackington Haven beach and glorious coastal footpath. Positively no bar, disco or bingo; just beautiful countryside. Facilities include free showers, laundry, baby bathroom, games/TV rooms and children's play area. Short drive from Bodmin Moor, fine surfing beaches like Widemouth Bay, the Camel Estuary for sailing, windsurfing, cycling and within easy reach of Padstow, Polzeath, Rock, etc. Many attractive country pubs locally, plenty of attractions for children. Caravan sales. Camping/touring £4.50 - £5.00 per adult per night. Pets welcome – dog walk on site and dog-friendly woods, beaches etc. within a 5 to 10 minute drive. Under new ownership.

e-mail: contact@hentervene.co.uk   **website: www.hentervene.co.uk**

HELSTON

Brian and Dawn Thompson, Franchis Holiday Park, Cury Cross Lanes, Mullion, Helston TR12 7AZ (01326 240301). A warm welcome awaits you at Franchis, centrally positioned on the Lizard Peninsula, where beaches, coves and cliff walks abound. Touring and camping or self-catering in our caravans or bungalows all surrounded by woodland and farmland. Four acres of closely mown grass. Electric hook-ups, hot showers, small licensed shop. No entertainment or bar. Dogs welcome. Wreck and reef diving nearby. **AA** *THREE PENNANTS.*
e-mail: enquiries@franchis.co.uk
website: www.franchis.co.uk

LOOE

Mr and Mrs G. Veale, Trelay Farmpark, Pelynt, Looe PL13 2JX (01503 220900). Trelay Farmpark is a small, peaceful, friendly, family-run site. It is quiet, uncommercialised and surrounded by farmland. The park lies on a gentle south-facing slope offering wide views of open countryside. Excellent new facilities include hot showers/ launderette and disabled suite with wheelchair access. The three-acre camping field is licensed for 55 tourers/tents etc. Good access, generous pitches, hook ups. In adjoining area (1.5 acres) are 20 holiday caravans in a garden-like setting. The nearby village of Pelynt has shops, Post Office, restaurants, pub. Looe and Polperro are both just three miles away. The renowned Eden Project is 12 miles west. Two new luxury caravans and two available for dog owners. Controlled dogs welcome. **ETC ★★★★**

🆂 🛖 **NEWQUAY**

Treloy Tourist Park, Newquay TR8 4JN (01637 872063/876279). A friendly family site for touring caravans, tents and motor homes, just off the A3059 Newquay Road. A central location for touring the whole of Cornwall. Facilities include heated swimming pool, licensed bar/family room, entertainment, cafe/takeaway, shop, laundry, FREE showers, private washing cubicles, baby bathrooms, indoor dishwashing sinks, TV and games rooms, adventure playground. Facilities for the disabled. Electric hook-ups. Terms £8 to £13 per night for two adults, car and caravan. Coarse fishing nearby. Own superb 9-hole Par 32 golf course with concessionary green fees for our guests. Please write or telephone for free colour brochure. **ETC ★★★★, AA** *THREE PENNANTS*.

🚐 🆂 🛖 **PENZANCE**

Mrs M. Maddock, Bone Valley Caravan and Camping Park, Heamoor, Penzance TR20 8UJ (Tel & Fax: 01736 360313). Situated in a pretty valley, ideal for exploring the countryside and coast of West Cornwall, this small quiet park is well sheltered by mature hedges and trees, and is bordered on one side by a small stream. 17 pitches (some hardstanding) as well as areas for small tents. Electric hook-ups. Caravans available for hire. The village of Heamoor with shops, pub and regular bus service is a short walk away. On-site facilities include showers, kitchen/laundry room (microwave, electric kettle), shop, take-away, bicycle hire, campers' lounge with colour TV, public telephone, free ice pack service, chemical disposal, gas and Camping Gaz and BBQ loan. **AA** *THREE PENNANTS*.
e-mail: bonevalleycandcpark@fsbdial.co.uk

REDRUTH

See also Colour Display Advertisement

🚐 🆂 🛖

Globe Vale Holiday Park, Radnor, Redruth TR16 4BH (01209 891183). Globe Vale is a quiet countryside park situated close to the town of Redruth and the main A30. There are panoramic views across green fields to the coast; 10 minutes' drive to the nearest beach. Campers/tourers; static caravans for hire, and also plots available if you wish to buy your own new static holiday home. Facilities on site include electric hook-ups, shower/toilet block, launderette and sluice. There is also a children's play area, and open spaces for ball games. We are happy to accept pets on site at extra charge. Contact **Paul and Louise Owen.**
website: www.globevale.co.uk

REDRUTH

When making enquiries please mention FHG Publications

ST IVES

G. & H. Rogers, Hellesveor Caravan and Camping Site, Hellesveor Farm, St Ives TR26 3AD (01736 795738). Six-berth caravans for hire on small secluded approved farm site, one mile from St Ives town centre and nearest beaches, five minutes from bus route on Land's End Road (B3306). Coastal and countryside walks nearby. Laundry facilities on site. Special terms for early and late season. Campers and touring caravans welcome. Electrical hook-ups available. Dogs allowed under strict control. Nearby horse riding, pony trekking, golf course, bowling greens and leisure centre. SAE for further details.

TINTAGEL

See also Colour Display Advertisement

Bossiney Farm Caravan & Touring Park, Bossiney, Tintagel PL34 0AY (01840 770481; Fax: 01840 770025) Family- run caravan and campsite renowned for its cleanliness and hospitality, situated on the coastal route between Tintagel and Boscastle in the historically interesting hamlet of Bossiney. Safe, sandy bay a short walk away. A range of modern luxury caravan homes (some new for 2005), to suit all needs, with a well equipped kitchen and everything you would expect on a modern caravan holiday. Also touring and camping pitches, many with electric hook-ups, on landscaped site with flat, sheltered terraces. Well appointed, bright and clean toilet block, with showers, hairdryers (token) and free hot water to hand basins and wash sinks. Well stocked shop, laundry, and baby changing and disabled facilities. Pets welcome. **ETC ★★★★.**
website: www.bossineyfarm.co.uk

ENGLAND — Ratings You Can Trust

The **English Tourism Council** (formerly the English Tourist Board) has joined with the **AA** and **RAC** to create a new, easily understood quality rating for serviced accommodation, giving a clear guide of what to expect.

HOTELS are given a rating from One to Five **Stars.**

GUEST ACCOMMODATION, which includes guest houses, bed and breakfasts, inns and farmhouses, is rated from One to Five **Diamonds**.

HOLIDAY PARKS, TOURING PARKS and CAMPING PARKS – standards of quality range from a One Star (acceptable) to a Five Star (exceptional) park.

SELF-CATERING – the more **Stars** (from One to Five) awarded to an establishment, the higher the levels of quality you can expect. Establishments at higher rating levels also have to meet some additional requirements for facilities.

SCOTLAND

Star Quality Grades will reflect the most important aspects of a visit, such as the warmth of welcome, efficiency and friendliness of service, the quality of the food and the cleanliness and condition of the furnishings, fittings and decor.

THE MORE STARS, THE HIGHER THE STANDARDS.

The description, such as Hotel, Guest House, Bed and Breakfast, Lodge, Holiday Park, Self-catering etc tells you the type of property and style of operation.

WALES

STAR QUALITY GUIDE FOR

HOTELS, GUEST HOUSES AND FARMHOUSES

SELF-CATERING ACCOMMODATION (Cottages, Apartments, Houses)

CARAVAN HOLIDAY HOME PARKS (Holiday Parks, Touring Parks, Camping Parks)

Places which score highly will have an especially welcoming atmosphere and pleasing ambience, high levels of comfort and guest care, and attractive surroundings enhanced by thoughtful design and attention to detail.

TRURO

Mr and Mrs C.R. Simpkins, Summer Valley Touring Park, Shortlanesend, Truro TR4 9DW (01872 277878). Situated just two miles from Truro, Cornwall's cathedral city, and ideally placed as a centre for touring all parts of Cornwall. This quiet, small, secluded site is only one-and-a-half miles from the main A30 and its central situation is advantageous for North Cornwall's beautiful surfing beaches and rugged Atlantic coast or Falmouth's quieter and placid fishing coves. Horse riding, fishing and golf are all available within easy distance. This compact site is personally supervised by the owners. Facilities include a toilet block with free hot water, washing cubicles, showers, shaving points, launderette, iron, hairdryer, etc; caravan electric hook-ups; children's play area. Licensed shop with dairy products, groceries, bread, confectionery, toys, Calor/Camping gas. Terms: two people, car, caravan/tent £7.50 to £10 per day. **ETC** ★★★★ *EXCELLENT,* **AA** *THREE PENNANTS AND ENVIRONMENTAL AWARD.*

WADEBRIDGE
See also Colour Display Advertisement

Gunvenna Touring Caravan and Camping Park, St Minver, Wadebridge PL27 6QN (01208 862405). The Park is a well drained site of level grassland on 10 acres commanding uninterrupted views of the countryside within five minutes' drive of safe, golden, sandy beaches. Local activities include golf, fishing, tennis, surfing and swimming, etc. Site facilities include two modern toilet and shower blocks, launderette and ironing room, children's play area, children's games room (9am to 10pm), barbecue area, dog exercise area, shop, telephone, etc. We also have a licensed Bar and indoor heated swimming pool. Please send for our colour brochure and tariff. **AA** *FOUR PENNANTS, RAC LISTED.*

CAMPING SITES

THE LIZARD

Henry's Campsite, The Lizard. A small, family-run, friendly camping site. Situated at the top of Caerthillian Valley with splendid sea views and spectacular sunsets. Coastal footpaths and both quiet or popular beaches close by. Shower facilities, toilets and fresh water taps. Prices from £5. Despite the secluded situation the village centre is only two minutes' walk away with fish and chips, pub, gifts, grocer, cafes and restaurant. Write to **J. Lyne, Caerthillian Farm, The Lizard, Helston TR12 7NX (01326 290596).**

ST AUSTELL

Bill & Anne Truscott, Court Farm Caravan and Camping, St Stephen, St Austell PL26 7LE (01726 822727; Fax: 01726 823684). Court Farm is set in thirty acres of peaceful pasture land, with four acres designated for touring caravans and tents, to a limit of twenty pitches, with 16 EHUs. The shower block has free hot showers, flush toilets, laundry facility, freezer, and dishwashing area. There is a chemical disposal point. We have a small coarse fishing lake, and an astronomical telescope for star-gazing, lectures by arrangement. Centrally based for beaches and all of Cornwall's attractions; the Eden Project and the Gardens of Heligan are each six miles away. Terms from £7.50 to £17.50 per night based on unit size. Dogs welcome. **ETC** ★★★
website: www.courtfarmcornwall.co.uk

Cumbria

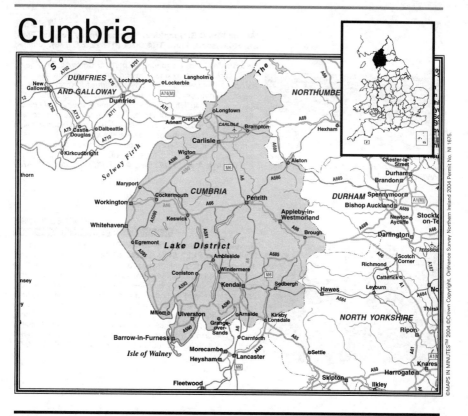

CARAVANS FOR HIRE

KESWICK

Causeway Foot Camping Barn. Situated two miles south-east of Keswick on a traditional Lakeland hill farm, with splendid views of Skiddaw, Blencathra and Helvellyn. This is one of the most picturesque and central locations in the Lake District. Available on an "exclusive use" basis, this two-storey barn has 20 bunkbeds with mattresses; a well-equipped kitchen, including fridge; microwave, gas cooker; electric lights and power points throughout. Toilets and showers are in a nearby building. At £4 per person per night, it provides a secure and economic base for groups on a budget. Long or short bookings taken. For further information please contact: **Greg Nicholson, Causeway Foot Farm, Naddle, Keswick, CA12 4TF (017687 72290).** **website: www.causewayfoot.co.uk**

LITTLE ASBY

Mrs M. Bainbridge, Whygill Head Farm, Little Asby, Appleby-in-Westmorland CA16 6QD (017683 71531). Two six-berth caravans on their own private site in half-acre sheltered copse near farm. Fully equipped except for bed linen. Electricity and running water, flush toilet and shower in both vans. Heating and cooking by Calor gas (no extra charge). Children welcome; also pets under control. An ideal centre for walkers and naturalists. Golf, fishing, swimming and pony trekking; interesting market towns and villages. Ideal for relaxation. Fell walking. Touring Yorkshire Dales and Lake District. Prices from £95 per week low season, £100 high season; weekends £15 per night.

PENRITH

John Burnett, Fell View Holidays, Grisedale Bridge, Glenridding, Penrith CA11 0PJ (Tel & Fax: 017684 82342, Evenings: 01768 867420). If peace and tranquillity combined with wonderful views are what you require for a good holiday then Fell View is the place for you. We are situated at the south end of Ullswater with only a field between us and the lake, with magnificent views of the surrounding fells. Our gardens and grounds, including the dog walk, are full of birds and flowers which everyone can enjoy. There is an abundance of walking, climbing and other outdoor activities all within easy reach. Also historic houses and gardens, and when the weather is inclement some interesting indoor attractions to visit. **website: www.fellviewholidays.com**

PENRITH

J Teasdale, Beckses Holiday Caravan Park, Penruddock, Penrith CA11 0RX (017684 83224). Conveniently situated within six miles of the M6 motorway, this caravan park offers a choice of holiday accommodation on the fringe of the Lake District National Park. Four and six-berth caravans for hire, with mains services, electric light and fridge, gas cooker and fire, toilet, separate double and bunk bedrooms, kitchen area and lounge. Fully equipped except linen. Alternatively those with touring caravans and tents will find excellent facilities on site; toilets, showers, chemical disposal points, stand pipes and laundry facilities. There is a play area with swings, etc, for children, also large recreation area. Within easy reach of outdoor heated swimming pool, pony trekking, fishing and fell walking. Some local pubs have restaurant facilities. Full details and terms on request. **AA** *THREE PENNANTS.*

Gleaston Water Mill

Ulverston, Cumbria • 01229 869244

website: www.gleastonmill.demon.co.uk

Working water-powered corn mill dating from the 1700s, with lots of interesting local artefacts. Traditional tea shop, country store, observation bee-hive.

🚐 📍 Å

PENRITH

Miss M. Lightfoot, Gillside Caravan & Camping Site, Gillside Farm, Glenridding, Penrith CA11 0QQ (017684 82346). Sited in an idyllic location above Ullswater, five minutes' walk from the village of Glenridding with shops, National Park Information Centre, post office, cafés and restaurants. The path to Helvellyn passes the farm. Well-equipped six-berth holiday homes; new bunkhouse, suitable for groups. Facilities include a constant supply of hot and cold water in the shower/toilet block, deep sinks for washing pots and pans and a laundry with washer/drier; electric hook-ups. Fresh milk and eggs available at the farmhouse. Activities include wind surfing, canoeing, sailing on the steamer, pony trekking and rock climbing. Open March to mid-November. Bunkhouse open all year.

e-mail: gillside@btconnect.com

website: www.gillsidecaravanandcampingsite.co.uk

HOLIDAY PARKS AND CENTRES

POOLEY BRIDGE/LAKE ULLSWATER

See also Colour Display Advertisement

🚐 📍 ☼ Å

Park Foot Caravan and Camping Park, Howtown Road, Pooley Bridge, Penrith CA10 2NA (017684 86309; Fax: 017684 86041). Park Foot Holiday Park combines an idyllic setting with so much to see and do. A family-run park catering for families and couples only, Park Foot offers touring caravan and camping pitches and self-catering cottages. All touring pitches have electricity and are close to a water point. Amenities include modern toilets with hot showers, laundry room, shop, direct access to Lake Ullswater and Barton Fell, two children's playgrounds, games and amusements, pony trekking, mountain bike hire, dog walking areas, licensed club with bar, restaurant and takeaways, disco, live entertainment and children's club in the summer season.

e-mail: holidays@parkfootullswater.co.uk

website: www.parkfootullswater.co.uk

ST BEES

See also Colour Display Advertisement

🚐 📍 Å

Seacote Park, The Beach, St Bees CA27 0ET (01946 822777; Fax: 01946 824442). Beside a lovely beach in an award-winning historic village on the fringe of the Lake District, an ideal centre for exploring the Western Lakes and Fells, headland walks, bird sanctuary, golf and indoor pool nearby. Modern, fully-equipped two and three bedroomed, centrally heated caravans for hire; large area for tourers and campers. On-site hotel, restaurant and bar; entertainment in season. Shop open seven days; laundry room and toilet block. Dogs allowed under control. Holiday homes also for sale. Open all year round.

e-mail: reception@seacote.com

website: www.seacote.com

SILLOTH

See also Colour Display Advertisement

🚐 ☼ 📍

Solway Holiday Village, Skinburness Drive, Silloth, Near Carlisle CA7 4QQ (016973 31236). Set in a 120-acre park on the Solway Firth, an Area of Outstanding Natural Beauty, close to the Lake District and the Scottish Borders. Facilities available on-site include 134 fully-furnished and equipped lodges and luxury caravans, large touring area with mains hook-ups, superb indoor leisure pool with spa, mini ten-pin bowling alley, football and netball, family entertainment and kiddies club, licensed clubs with dancing and entertainment, themed bars, Peg's Kitchen Restaurant and Take-away, amusement arcade with pool, mini-market with fresh food and gifts, 9-hole par 3 golf course, sauna, sunbeds and gym, tennis courts, novelty train and children's play area. Everything you could ever need for a fun-filled family holiday.

e-mail: Solway@hagansleisure.co.uk

website: www.hagansleisure.co.uk

CARAVAN SITES AND NIGHT HALTS

🚐 ⛺

BRAMPTON

Mrs O.R. Campbell, Irthing Vale Caravan Park, Old Church Lane, Brampton, Near Carlisle CA8 2AA (016977 3600). Popular with tourists whose prime concern is cleanliness, peace and quiet, with the personal attention of the owner, this four-and-a-half acre park has pitches for 20 touring caravans, motorised caravans plus space for camping. There is a small site shop, laundry room, mains water and drainage and electric hook-ups. In fact all the amenities one would expect on a quiet, modern caravan park. We are very close to Hadrian's (Roman) Wall and convenient for having days out discovering romantic Scottish Border country. The ideal site for walking, sailing, fishing and golf. Open 1st March until 31st October. Terms from £9 per car/caravan plus two persons. Special reductions for hikers and cyclists. **AA ★★★**, *AA THREE PENNANTS, CARAVAN AND CAMPING CLUB LISTED SITE.*
e-mail: glennwndrby@aol.com   **website: www.ukparks.co.uk/irthingvale**

🚐 🚐 ⛺

GRANGE-OVER-SANDS

Greaves Farm Caravan Park, Field Broughton, Grange-over-Sands. Family-run, small quiet grass site with luxury six berth caravans. Fully serviced. Colour TV, fridge. Equipped except for linen. Tourers and tents welcome. Two miles north of Cartmel, two miles south of foot of Lake Windermere. Convenient base for touring Lake District. Personal supervision. Open March to October. SAE for details to **Mrs E. Rigg, Prospect House, Barber Green, Grange-over-Sands LA11 6HU (015395 36329 or 36587).** ETC ★★★★

🚐 ⛺

KENDAL

Waters Edge Caravan Park, Milnthorpe, Near Kendal LA7 7NN (015395 67708). Modern purpose-built park with top class amenities just three-quarters of a mile from M6 Exit 36. Within easy reach of the Lakes, Yorkshire Dales, West Coast and Morecambe Bay. With licensed lounge bar, off-licence, TV lounge, pool table, facilities for the disabled, sunbed, shop, Calor gas, barbecues, picnic tables, fully tiled private showers, toilets and wash cubicles, laundry and washing up facilities all with free hot water. All hardstanding pitches with electric hook-ups. Many suitable for awnings. Luxury two, four and six-berth Motorhomes for hire. Please telephone or write for our free colour brochure. Call for bar opening times. ETC ★★★★

🚐 ⛺

KESWICK

Linda Lamb, Burns Caravan & Camping Site, St Johns in the Vale CA12 4RR (01768 779225). Quiet family-run caravan and camping site, situated two-and-a-half miles east of Keswick-on-Derwentwater. Beautiful views of the surrounding fells. Ideal centre for walking and touring the Lake District. Touring caravans, motor caravans and tents are welcome. Electric hook-ups are available. Toilet block with hot showers etc. Prices from £10 per caravan inclusive of electric hook-up and from £8 per tent. Enquiries with S.A.E. please to **Mrs Linda Lamb.** *AA THREE PENNANTS.*
e-mail: info@burnsfarmcamping.co.uk

🚐 🚐 ⛺

NEWBY BRIDGE

Oak Head Caravan Park, Ayside, Grange-over-Sands LA11 6JA (015395 31475). Family-owned and operated. Select, quiet, clean, wooded site in the picturesque fells of the Lake District. Easy access from M6 Junction 36, 14 miles A590. On-site facilites include flush toilets, hot showers, hot and cold water, deep sinks for washing clothes, washing machine, tumble dryers and spin dryers, hair dryers, iron and deep freeze. Gas on sale. Tourers (30 pitches) £10 per night (including electricity and VAT). Tents (30 pitches) £8.50 per night, £10 on electricity, up to four persons. Open March 31st to October 31st.

📷 §

Tanglewood Caravan Park, Causeway Head, Silloth-on-Solway CA7 4PE (016973 31253). Tanglewood is a family-run park on the fringes of the Lake District National Park. It is tree-sheltered and situated one mile inland from the small port of Silloth on the Solway Firth, with a beautiful view of the Galloway Hills. Large modern holiday homes are available from March to January, with car parking beside each home. Fully equipped except for bed linen, with end bedroom, panel heaters in both bedrooms and bathroom, electric lighting, hot and cold water, toilet, shower, gas fire, fridge and colour TV, all of which are included in the tariff. Touring pitches also available with electric hook-ups and water/drainage facilities, etc. Play area. Licensed lounge with adjoining children's play room. Pets welcome free but must be kept under control at all times. Full colour brochure available. ★★★, **AA** *THREE PENNANTS.*
e-mail: tanglewoodcaravanpark@hotmail.com   **website: www.tanglewoodcaravanpark.co.uk**

CAMPING SITES

⛺

PENRITH

R & A Taylforth, Side Farm, Patterdale, Penrith CA11 0NP (017684 82337). Camping on the shores of Lake Ullswater for tents and motor caravans (sorry, no towing caravans), surrounded by the beautiful scenery of the Lake District. Activities on the lake include swimming, sailing, boating, canoeing and fishing; steamer cruises. Modern toilet block, showers, washing facilities, shaving, hair drying points, washing machines and dryers. Dogs allowed provided they are kept on a lead. Convenient for touring the Lake District National Park. Fresh milk and eggs are available at the farm, with shops and post office in nearby Patterdale; regular bus services. Terms - Adults £4.50 per night; reductions for children; vehicles/motor bikes £1, boats/trailers 50p. Open Easter to November.

⛺

Waterside House Campsite, Waterside House, Howtown Road, Pooley Bridge, Penrith CA10 2NA (Tel & Fax: 017684 86332). Farm and campsite situated about one mile from Pooley Bridge. Genuine Lakeside location with beautiful views of Lake Ullswater and Fells. Ideal for windsurfing, canoeing, boating, fell walking and fishing, table tennis, volleyball. Boat, canoe and mountain bike hire on site. Play area, shop and gas exchange also. SAE or telephone for brochure. Open March to October. Directions: M6 Junction 40, A66 follow signs for Ullswater, A592 to Pooley Bridge, one mile along Howtown Road on right - signposted. **ETC** ★★★★
e-mail: enquire@watersidefarm-campsite.co.uk
website: www.watersidefarm-campsite.co.uk

📷 § ⛺

Cove Caravan & Camping Park, Watermillock, Penrith, Cumbria CA11 0LS (017684 86549). Cove Park is a peaceful caravan and camping park overlooking Lake Ullswater, surrounded by Fells with beautiful views. The park is very well maintained with a five star and 'Excellent' ETC rating. We are ideally situated for walking, watersports and all of the Lake District tourist attractions in the North Lakes. Facilities include clean heated showers and washrooms with hand and hair dryers, washing and drying machines, iron and board, and a separate washing up area, hot drinks machine and a freezer for ice packs. We offer electric hook-ups with hardstandings, and plenty of sheltered grass for campers. Luxury holiday home available to rent. **ETC** ★★★★★, **AA** *THREE PENNANTS.*
website: www.cove-park.co.uk

Derbyshire

CARAVANS FOR HIRE

ASHBOURNE
See also Colour Display Advertisement

Arthur Tatlow, Ashfield Farm, Calwich, Near Ashbourne DE6 2EB (01335 324279 or 324443). Working farm. Five modern six-berth caravans, fully equipped, each with gas cooker, fridge, TV; shower and flush toilet; mains electricity. Ashfield Farm overlooks the peaceful Dove Valley and is convenient for the Peak District. The old market town of Ashbourne is only two miles away, with golf courses, swimming pool, squash and bowling. Within easy reach of stately homes like Haddon Hall and Chatsworth, with the Potteries and Lichfield 25 miles distant, Uttoxeter 10 miles away while Alton Towers Theme Park is under five miles away. Prices and brochure on request. Write or telephone for further information.

CARAVAN SITES AND NIGHT HALTS

BUXTON (near)
See also Colour Display Advertisement

Newhaven Caravan and Camping Park, Newhaven, Near Buxton SK17 0DT (01298 84300). Delightful site in the heart of the Peak District providing an ideal centre for touring the Derbyshire Dales, walking, climbing, potholing, etc. Convenient for visiting Chatsworth, Haddon House, Hardwick House, Alton Towers, Matlock and the Dams. Two first class toilet blocks providing FREE hot water; electric hook-ups. Children's playground, playroom, fully-stocked shop supplying Calor and Camping gas, fresh groceries, etc. Laundry. Ice pack freezing facilities. Restaurant adjacent. Tents, motor vans, caravans. Pets and children welcome. Terms from £8.50 per night - includes car and up to four people, discount for seven nights or more. SAE for brochure. Seasonal tourers welcome. **ETC ★★★, AA** *THREE PENNANTS.*

Devon

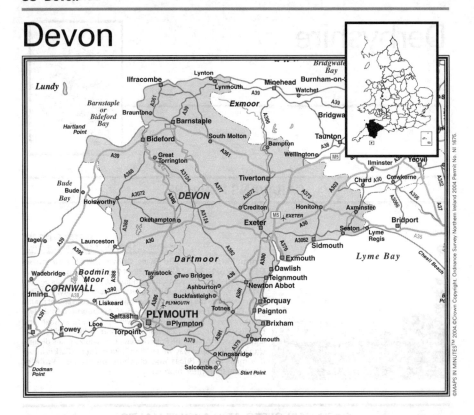

CARAVANS FOR HIRE

 BRANSCOMBE

Mrs A.E. White, Berry Barton, Branscombe, Near Seaton EX12 3BD (01297 680208; Fax: 01297 680108). Our park stands above the picturesque old village of Branscombe with thatched cottages, bakery museum and smithy. There are two freehouses in the village, the nearest within easy walking distance. We offer a quiet, peaceful holiday for both retired people and families; there is a large area for children to play. The site is on our 300 acre dairy and mixed farm, with one mile of coastline. Riding available nearby. There are many lovely walks with golf and fishing within easy reach, as are Seaton and Sidmouth (5 miles), the fishing village of Beer (3 miles), and the motorway (17 miles). Six-berth caravans available from March to November. Mains water; flush toilets; mains electricity; colour TV; fridge. All caravans have toilets; showers and hot water.

COLYTON

Bonehayne Farm, Colyton EX24 6SG. Working farm. Enjoy a relaxing holiday deep in the tranquil Devon countryside. Bonehayne is a 250 acre family farm. Our six-berth luxury caravan is situated in the farmhouse garden. It is south-facing and overlooks the banks of the River Coly. It is quiet and tranquil and the caravan enjoys lovely surrounding views. Two miles from the quaint little town of Colyton; four miles to coast. Children welcome – we have spacious lawns and animals to see. Good trout fishing, woodlands and walks. Laundry room, picnic tables, barbecue, deck chairs. Bed and Breakfast also available. Details from **Mrs R. Gould (01404 871396)** or **Mrs S. Gould (01404 871416)**
e-mail: gould@bonehayne.co.uk
website: www.bonehayne.co.uk

COMBE MARTIN

Manleigh Holiday Park, Combe Martin EX34 0NS (01271 883353). Quiet family-run site set in beautiful countryside near village, beaches, rocky coves and Exmoor. Chalets and caravans for hire. Swimming pool, children's play area, laundry. Scenic dog walk. New for 2005 - bistro serving delicious home-made food. Colour brochure: **L Whitney. ETC ★★★★ website: www.manleighholidaypark.co.uk**

CULLOMPTON

Mrs A. M. Davey, Pound Farm, Butterleigh, Cullompton EX15 1PH (01884 855208). Working farm. Sleeps 7. Enjoy a family break all year round on this family-run 80 acre beef and sheep farm. At Pound Farm, a holiday combines typical English scenery with the traditional beauty of the village of Butterleigh. Our luxury two bedroomed static caravan with decking can accommodate up to seven people. One double bedroom, second bedroom has two single beds with a bunk above, both rooms have electric heating. Dining seating area can be made into a double bed. Kitchen has fridge, electric hob and double oven with grill. Bathroom, flushable toilet and handbasin; shower room with additional washbasin. Lounge has TV with teletext and electric fire. Iron, ironing board, kettle, toaster, all utensils, cutlery and crockery are provided free of charge. Adjacent outbuilding/utility room is ideal for storage of fishing gear and bait. The caravan is set within its own grass and gravelled area, with parking space for two cars. Visitors are free to walk over the farm. Pets welcome. Free fishing on Pound Farm during your stay, no closed season, well stocked with carp, tench, rudd and perch. North and South coast 40 - 60 minutes' drive. Four miles from M5 (Junction 28) Cullompton. Terms from £100 to £210 per week.

MODBURY

R.A. Blackler, Pennymoor Camping and Caravan Park, Modbury PL21 0SB (Tel & Fax: 01548 830542; Tel: 01548 830020). Immaculately maintained, well-drained, peaceful rural site with panoramic views. Midway between Plymouth and Kingsbridge (A379), it makes an ideal centre for touring. Central for moors, towns and beaches, only five miles from Bigbury-on-Sea and nine miles from Salcombe. Golf courses at Bigbury and Thurlestone and boating at Salcombe, Newton Ferrers and Kingsbridge. Large superb toilet/shower block with fully tiled walls and floors. Facilities for the disabled holidaymaker. Dishwashing room - FREE hot water. Laundry room. Play area specially equipped for children. Shop. Gas. Public telephone on site. Luxury caravans for hire, all services, fully equipped including colour TV. Ideal for touring caravans and tents. Write or phone for free colour brochure. **ETC ★★★★, AA** *THREE PENNANTS,* **RAC.**
e-mail: enquiries@pennymoor-camping.co.uk   website: www.pennymoor-camping.co.uk

SEATON
See also Colour Display Advertisement

Axevale Caravan Park, Seaton EX12 2DF (0800 0688816). A quiet, family-run park with 68 modern and luxury caravans for hire. The park overlooks the delightful River Axe Valley, and is just a 10 minute walk from the town with its wonderfully long, award-winning beach. Children will love our extensive play area, with its sand pit, paddling pool, swings and slide. Laundry facilities are provided and there is a wide selection of goods on sale in the park shop which is open every day. All of our caravans have a shower, toilet, fridge and TV. Also, with no clubhouse, a relaxing atmosphere is ensured. Prices from £80 per week; reductions for three or fewer persons early/late. **ETC ★★★
website: www.axevale.co.uk**

TAVISTOCK

🚐 💲 🛡

Harford Bridge Holiday Park, Peter Tavy, Tavistock PL19 9LS (01822 810349; Fax: 01822 810028). Beautiful sheltered park set in Dartmoor beside the River Tavy, with delightful views of Cox Tor. Just two miles from Tavistock off the A386 Okehampton Road, take Peter Tavy turn. Riverside camping and other level spacious pitches - free hot water and showers. Open end March till November. Self-catering luxury caravan holiday homes, centrally heated and double glazed for winter letting - includes all bedding, heat and light. Open all year. Children's play area, tennis and table tennis, fly fishing, dog exercise field, parking beside units. Nearby pony-trekking and golf. ETC ★★★★, *DAVID BELLAMY GOLD AWARD, ROSE AWARD 2004, BH&HPA.* **e-mail: enquiry@harfordbridge.co.uk** **website: www.harfordbridge.co.uk**

WOOLACOMBE

🚐 💲 🛡

NORTH MORTE FARM CARAVAN & CAMPING PARK

North Morte Farm Caravan and Camping, Dept FHG, Mortehoe, Woolacombe EX34 7EG (01271 870381). The nearest camping and caravan park to the sea, in perfectly secluded beautiful coastal country. Our family-run park, adjoining National Trust land, is only 500 yards from Rockham Beach, yet only five minutes' walk from the village of Mortehoe with a post office, petrol station/garage, shops, cafes and pubs – one which has a children's room. Four to six berth holiday caravans for hire and pitches for tents, dormobiles and touring caravans, electric hook-ups available. We have hot showers and flush toilets, laundry room, shop and off licence; Calor gas and Camping Gaz available; children's play area. Dogs accepted but must be kept on lead. Open Easter to end September. Brochure available. ETC ★★★★

HOLIDAY PARKS AND CENTRES

🚐 ☼ 💲 🛡

ASHBURTON

Parkers Farm Holidays Park, Ashburton TQ13 7LJ (01364 652598; Fax: 01364 654004). A friendly, family-run farm site set in 400 acres and surrounded by beautiful countryside. 12 miles to the sea and close to Dartmoor National Park; ideal for touring Devon/Cornwall. Perfect for children and pets with all farm animals, play area and plenty of space to roam, also large area for dogs. Holiday cottages and caravans, fully equipped except for linen. Level touring site with some hard standings. Free showers in fully tiled block, laundry room, games room. Small family bar, restaurant, shop and phone. Prices start from £90 Low Season to £480 High Season. Good discounts for couples. To find us, take the A38 to Plymouth till you see "26 miles Plymouth" sign. Take second left at Alston Cross signposted to Woodland and Denbury. ETC ★★★★, *AA FOUR PENNANTS; BRITISH FARM TOURIST AWARD. 2004 GOLD AWARD FOR QUALITY AND SERVICE. ROSE AWARD 2005. SILVER DAVID BELLAMY CONSERVATION AWARD. PRACTICAL CARAVAN TOP 100 PARKS 2004.* **e-mail: parkersfarm@btconnect.com** **website: www.parkersfarm.co.uk**

CHALLABOROUGH
See also Colour Display Advertisement

Challaborough Bay Holiday Park (01548 810771). Offering direct access to an award-winning sandy beach and stunning views across to Burgh Island. Indoor heated swimming pool, kids' club and family entertainment. For a free colour brochure or to make a booking call **Parkdean Holidays** on **0870 420 5607.** ETC ★★★★
e-mail: **enquiries@parkdeanholidays.co.uk**
website: **www.parkdeanholidays.co.uk**

CROYDE BAY
See also Colour Display Advertisement

Ruda Holiday Park, Croyde Bay (01271 890671). Ruda is set at the centre of seven miles of Croyde Bay's glorious sands. A fabulous choice of accommodation from lodges, caravans, apartments and camping pitches. Indoor heated pool, kids' clubs and live entertainment. For a free colour brochure or to make a booking call **Parkdean Holidays** on **0870 420 5607.** ETC ★★★★, **AA** *HOLIDAY CENTRE.*
e-mail: **enquiries@parkdeanholidays.co.uk**
website: **www.ruda.co.uk**

WOOLACOMBE

Beach Road, Woolacombe
North Devon, EX34 7AN
Bookings: 01271 871425

Early Bookings 10% Discount!

www.europapark.co.uk

Camping and Touring
We have beautiful landscaped Camping and Touring pitches, all overlooking Woolacombe Beach & Lundy Island. Electric Pitches and All Service pitches are available.

Site Accommodation
Luxury wooden lodges, Bungalows, Static Caravans, Cabins & Chalets available sleeping from 4 - 8 people.

Facilities
Restaurant, Clubhouse, Indoor Swimming Pool, Sauna, Launderette, SPAR Market.

Special Area - For Young People & Large Groups. *Open All Year!*

Best Views in Woolacombe - "Probably!"

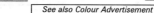
See also Colour Advertisement

Woolacombe Bay Holiday Parcs, Woolacombe EX34 7HW (01271 870 343 8am - 10pm 7 days). FUN FILLED HOLIDAYS ON THE GLORIOUS GOLDEN COAST! Choose from four fantastic holiday parcs - all beside the biggest Blue Flag beach in Devon. Luxury lodges, apartments and holiday homes in superb settings, plus excellent camping and touring pitches and facilities in delightful National Trust surroundings. Our own bars and restaurants are nearby so you can eat out and have fun every night. Friendly, caring staff and a family-run business ensure your holiday at Woolacombe Bay is very special and you'll always be made welcome. 10-pin bowling, golf club, crèche, 17th century inn, restaurants. PLUS FREE - 10 pools, nightly entertainment, water slides, health suite, tennis, kids' indoor and outdoor play areas, kids' club, plus much more! **ETC ★★★★**, *DAVID BELLAMY CONSERVATION GOLD AWARD.*
website: www.woolacombe.com

WOOLACOMBE

HOLIDAY PARCS
Fun Filled Holidays
ON DEVON'S GLORIOUS GOLDEN COAST

See our advert
on the back
cover for
full details.

01271 870 343
www.woolacombe.com
WOOLACOMBE • NORTH DEVON • EX34 7HW

FREE or REDUCED RATE entry to Holiday Visits and Attractions
— see our READERS' OFFER VOUCHERS on pages 41-68

World of Country Life
Exmouth, Devon • 01395 274533
website: www.worldofcountrylife.co.uk
All-weather attraction with Victorian street, vintage cars, indoor play area, pets centre, safari deer train, plus lots more. Something for all the family!

CARAVAN SITES AND NIGHT HALTS

AXMINSTER

See also Colour Display Advertisement

Hunters Moon Country Estate, Wareham Road, Hawkchurch EX13 5UL (01297 678402; Fax: 01297 678720). Embracing the splendour of the World Heritage Jurassic Coastline. A quality family park with panoramic views over the beautiful Axe Valley, offering static/touring/camping holidays. Positioned on the Devon/ Dorset border and conveniently located near West Bay, Lyme Regis and Seaton. Seasonal touring pitches available. Rallies welcome. Luxury static homes for sale. Dogs welcome. **ETC** ★★★★
e-mail: enquiries@huntersmooncountryestate.co.uk
website: www.huntersmooncountryestate.co.uk

BARNSTAPLE

See also Colour Display Advertisement

Tarka Holiday Park, Ashford, Barnstaple EX31 4AU (01271 343691 – Reservations). Caravans by the Taw Estuary in glorious North Devon. A splendid place to spend your holiday. Overlooking the magnificent Taw Estuary with the famous Tarka Trail opposite, our Holiday Park is centrally situated and is only minutes away from some of the country's finest 'Blue Flag' beaches. Close to many of North Devon's superb attractions,Tarka Holiday Park is on a direct route to Croyde, Ilfracombe and Woolacombe. Modern Holiday Caravans with full facilities for self-catering with separate fields for Tourers and Campers. Shower blocks and laundry area are centrally sited. **AA** *THREE PENNANTS. DAVID BELLAMY SILVER AWARDS.*
e-mail: info@tarkaholidaypark.co.uk
website: www.tarkaholidaypark.co.uk

CHUDLEIGH

See also Colour Display Advertisement

Holmans Wood Holiday Park, Chudleigh TQ13 0DZ (01626 853785, Fax: 01626 853792). Delightful personally managed park set back in secluded wooded area. Easily accessed from the A38 and ideally situated for Dartmoor and Haldon Forest. Close to Exeter, Plymouth and Torquay, and sandy beaches at Dawlish and Teignmouth. Trout and coarse fishing, golf, horse riding and bird watching are nearby. Our facilities include some hardstandings, electric hook-ups, excellent toilets/showers including disabled toilet. Seasonal pitches, meadow for camping, storage available and holiday homes for sale. Rallies welcome. Credit card facility for telephone bookings. **ETC** ★★★★, **AA** *THREE PENNANTS.*
e-mail: enquiries@holmanswood.co.uk
website: www.holmanswood.co.uk

COMBE MARTIN

See also Colour Display Advertisement

Stowford Farm Meadows Touring Caravan and Camping Park, Berry Down, Combe Martin EX34 0PW (01271 882476; Fax: 01271 883053). Set in 500 acres of glorious Devon countryside, and on the western edge of Exmoor National Park, this site has a superb rural setting. Renowned as a high quality park, offering outstanding value and service. Facilities include four modern luxury amenity blocks, laundry facilities, the old stable bars and indoor heated swimming pool. Shop, snooker, games room, horse riding, golf, sports field, undercover mini-zoo, petorama, crazy golf, kiddies kars and cycle hire. Extensive nature walks in mature woodland. Superb choice of five local beaches. Low season special offer - one week for £38 including electricity, Mid season - £58. Caravan storage available, seasonal pitches. Caravan workshop, repairs and accessories. Please telephone for a free colour brochure. **ETC** ★★★★, **AA** *FOUR PENNANTS.*
e-mail: enquiries@stowford.co.uk   website: www.stowford.co.uk

Caravan & Camping Park

EXMOUTH

Jon and Sue Tansley, St John's Farm Caravan & Camping Park, St Johns Road, Withycombe, Exmouth EX8 5EG (01395 263170). Our unique situation away from the hustle and bustle of the main town of Exmouth is ideal for those seeking a little peace and quiet, yet is ideally situated as a base to explore all the things that Devon is famous for, including Orcombe Point, the start of the East Devon Heritage Coast. The caravan park and camp site is situated in pleasant pasture land with rural views, yet only minutes away from two miles for glorious sandy beaches or unspoilt heathland. Stop overnight, spend a weekend with us, or stay for a month! Whatever you choose you will be assured of a warm Devonshire welcome at this family-run site. Facilities include: farm/site shop, electric hook-ups, toilets/disabled facilities, free showers, hairdryers, water points, children's playground, pets corner and bicycles for hire. Dogs welcome - exercise area available.
e-mail: st.johns.farm@amserve.net

KINGSBRIDGE
See also Colour Display Advertisement

Mounts Farm Touring Park, The Mounts, Near East Allington, Kingsbridge TQ9 7QJ (01548 521591). Mounts Farm is a family-run site in the heart of South Devon. On-site facilities include FREE hot showers, flush toilets, FREE hot water in washing-up room, razor points, laundry and information room, electric hook-ups and site shop. We welcome tents, touring caravans and motor caravans. Large pitches in level, sheltered fields. No charges for awnings. Children and pets welcome. Situated three miles north of Kingsbridge, Mounts Farm is an ideal base for exploring Dartmouth, Salcombe, Totnes, Dartmoor and the many safe, sandy beaches nearby. Please telephone or write for a free brochure. Self-catering cottage also available.
website: www.mountsfarm.co.uk

KINGSBRIDGE

Mr P. W. Shepherd, Alston Farm, Malborough, Kingsbridge TQ7 3BJ (Tel & Fax: 01548 561260). The family-run site is set in a quiet secluded, sheltered valley adjoining the Salcombe Estuary in amongst Devon's loveliest countryside. Level pitches, ample space and conveniences. Dish washing and clothes washing facilities. Electric hook-ups, Calor and Gaz stockists. Shop, (high season only), payphone on site. Children and pets welcome. Terms from £8 per night for two adults and caravan. Please phone for brochure: **Phil Shepherd.**
e-mail: alston.campsite@ukgateway.net   **website: www.welcome.to/alstonfarm**

OKEHAMPTON (near)

Olditch Farm Holiday Park, Sticklepath, Near Okehampton EX20 2NT (01837 840734; Fax: 01837 840877). Olditch is a small family-run site within Dartmoor National Park. Tourers, tents and motorhomes welcome, also holiday homes for hire. With direct access to the Moor, we are an ideal base for walking or letterboxing. Ideal base for touring Devon with easy access to both coasts. We welcome well-behaved dogs and have a small children's play area. Several good pubs (ale and food) and local shops within walking distance. Open March to November. Terms from £10 per night. **ETC ★★★, AA** *THREE PENNANTS*.
e-mail: stay@olditch.co.uk
website: www.olditch.co.uk

SALCOMBE

Sun Park Caravan and Camping, Soar Mill Cove, Salcombe TQ7 3DS (01548 561378). Peaceful, family-run site set amidst National Trust land. Within walking distance of sandy cove and coastal footpath. Fully equipped modern caravans with all facilities and some with sea views. Well equipped laundry room; new children's wooden adventure playground and TV/games room. Spacious level camping field, electric hook-ups, fully refurbished shower/toilet block. Outdoor activities to suit all interests and ages nearby. Open Easter to September. Brochure on request. **AA** *THREE PENNANTS.*
website: www.sun-park.co.uk

SANDY BAY

See also Colour Display Advertisement

Devon Cliffs, Sandy Bay, Exmouth. Luxury two and three bedroom caravans all with sea views. Colour TV, fridge, microwave, gas fire and cooker, shower and toilet. Indoor and outdoor heated swimming and fun pools. Clubs and children's entertainment, shops, restaurants and takeaways, sandy beach. Dogs welcome in some caravans. Further details available from **Mrs B. Love, 13 Claremont Road, Bishopston, Bristol BS7 8DL (Tel & Fax: 0117 924 3807; mobile: 07970 042054).**

SIDMOUTH

See also Colour Display Advertisement

Salcombe Regis Camping and Caravan Park, Salcombe Regis, Sidmouth EX10 0JH (01395 514303; Fax: 01395 514314). Ten luxuriously equipped leisure homes for hire. Spacious level park with sea views, within walking distance of the sea. Tranquil setting with excellent touring facilities. Superb walking country. Sidmouth's closest Gold Award-winning holiday park in an Area of Outstanding Natural Beauty. Under the personal supervision of resident proprietors, **Neil & Lesley Hook. ETC ★★★★★, AA** *THREE PENNANTS, DAVID BELLAMY GOLD AWARD 1996, ROSE AWARD PARK, BHHPA.*
e-mail: info@salcombe-regis.co.uk
website: www.salcombe-regis.co.uk

Dorset

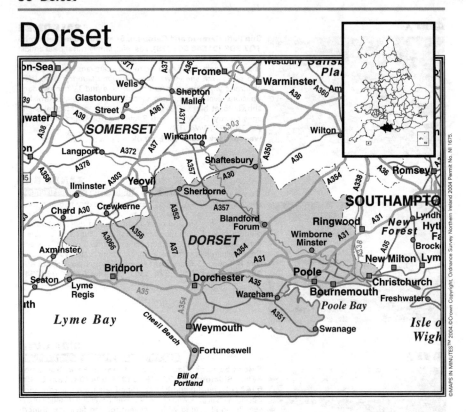

CARAVANS FOR HIRE

BRIDPORT

Eype House Caravan Park, Eype, Bridport DT6 6AL (01308 424903). A small quiet family-run park in an Area of Outstanding Natural Beauty. The park lies on the Coastal Path and is just 200 yards from the beach, making it ideal for walkers and the less energetic. Static vans for hire from £160 to £400 per week depending on size and season. All tent pitches are terraced and have wonderful sea views. Tent charges £8 to £14 per night. Sorry, no touring vans. Children and dogs welcome.

DORCHESTER (near)

Home Farm, Rectory Lane, Puncknowle, Near Dorchester DT2 9BW (01308 897258). Small secluded site in beautiful area, one-and-a-half-miles from West Bexington, four miles from Abbotsbury and Burton Bradstock. We can accommodate tents, touring caravans, and motor caravans. Facilities include mains water, washbasins, showers, razor points, disposal point for chemical toilets, electric hook-ups; gas. There is also a caravan for hire. Sea fishing available locally. Good food served at the village inn. Children and pets welcome. Further information on request.

REDLANDS FARM CARAVAN PARK

...for Personal Service and Easiest Access to Weymouth Beach...

Very conveniently situated in a semi-rural location backing onto open fields, yet not too far from the town centre and 1½ miles from the seafront. Buses stop just outside the park entrance and serve not only the town centre but much of Dorset. Ideal for day trips exploring the lovely countryside.

- Thirty 4 - 8 berth modern luxury caravans for hire with all services plus colour TV and fridge
- Friendly family-run park • Launderette facilities • Supermarkets close by • Personal supervision
- Caravan sales • Children and Pets welcome • Plenty of official footpaths and country walks to explore • Car parking alongside caravans • Open March to October
- Terms per week £150 - £440

SAE for enquiries.

REDLANDS FARM CARAVAN PARK

DORCHESTER ROAD, WEYMOUTH, DORSET DT3 5AP

Tel: 01305 812291 • Fax: 01305 814251

Redlands Sports Club is opposite the park where club, bar and sports facilities are available. Membership open to all visitors.

See also Colour Advertisement.

• • Some Useful Guidance for Guests and Hosts • •

Every year literally thousands of holidays, short breaks and overnight stops are arranged through our guides, the vast majority without any problems at all. In a handful of cases, however, difficulties do arise about bookings, which often could have been prevented from the outset.

It is important to remember that when accommodation has been booked, both parties – guests and hosts – have entered into a form of contract. We hope that the following points will provide helpful guidance.

GUESTS:
- When enquiring about accommodation, be as precise as possible. Give exact dates, numbers in your party and the ages of any children.
- State the number and type of rooms wanted and also what catering you require – bed and breakfast, full board etc. Make sure that the position about evening meals is clear – and about pets, reductions for children or any other special points.
- Read our reviews carefully to ensure that the proprietors you are going to contact can supply what you want. Ask for a letter confirming all arrangements, if possible.
- If you have to cancel, do so as soon as possible. Proprietors do have the right to retain deposits and under certain circumstances to charge for cancelled holidays if adequate notice is not given and they cannot re-let the accommodation.

HOSTS:
- Give details about your facilities and about any special conditions. Explain your deposit system clearly and arrangements for cancellations, charges etc. and whether or not your terms include VAT.
- If for any reason you are unable to fulfil an agreed booking without adequate notice, you may be under an obligation to arrange suitable alternative accommodation or to make some form of compensation.

While every effort is made to ensure accuracy, we regret that FHG Publications cannot accept responsibility for errors, omissions or misrepresentations in our entries or any consequences thereof. Prices in particular should be checked because we go to press early. We will follow up complaints but cannot act as arbiters or agents for either party.

HOLIDAY PARKS AND CENTRES

🚐 🈂️ ☼ ⚠️

West Bay Holiday Park, near Bridport (01308 422424). Located right in the heart of West Bay, with the harbour, beach and village right on your doorstep, this park offers you all you need for a relaxing family holiday. Indoor heated pool, kids' clubs and live entertainment. For a free colour brochure or to make a booking call **Parkdean Holidays** on **0870 420 5607**. ETC ★★★★, **AA** *HOLIDAY CENTRE.*
e-mail: enquiries@parkdeanholidays.co.uk
website: www.parkdeanholidays.co.uk

🚐 🈂️ ⚠️

BRIDPORT

Highlands End Holiday Park, Eype, Bridport DT6 6AR (01308 422139; Fax: 01308 425672). Select family holiday park with exceptional views of Lyme Bay and West Dorset "World Heritage" coastline. Indoor swimming pool; bar and restaurant with display of Fire Service memorabilia. Surrounded by countryside and the coast, the park is an ideal location for touring the area or walking the many coastal and inland footpaths. Our 5-star facilities provide you with the standard necessary for you to enjoy your break in West Dorset. Please visit our website for more information and photographs. ETC ★★★★★, *DAVID BELLAMY GOLD AWARD*
e-mail: holidays@wdlh.co.uk   **website: www.wdlh.co.uk**

🚐 ☼

Cobb's Holiday Park, 32 Gordon Road, Highcliffe-on-Sea, Christchurch BH23 5HN (01425 273301/275313; Fax: 01425 276090). Pleasant family-run park on a three-and-a-half acre site, with enviable location near New Forest and beaches. All caravans and chalets are full facility with free gas and electricity. We have a well provisioned shop, launderette, children's playground with rubber tiled safety surface, and licensed club with entertainment, free membership. Children and pets welcome. Open Easter to October. 45 static vans, 19 chalets available for hire. Terms - Caravans from £220 to £515, Chalets from £220 to £480. **ETC ★★★★** *ROSE AWARD, DAVID BELLAMY SILVER AWARD, CHRISTCHURCH IN BLOOM AWARD WINNER.*

🚐 🈂️ ☼ ⚠️

R. J. Verge & Mrs C. P. Knowles, Ulwell Farm Caravan Park, Ulwell, Swanage BH19 3DG. An attractive, small family-run park on a south-facing slope at the foot of the Purbeck Hills. Good base for walking, golf, riding, fishing and watersports. Six-berth caravans for hire from £100 to £425 per week. Children and pets welcome. Open April to September inclusive. Short Breaks available. For free colour brochure please write or phone **01929 422825**. ETC ★★★★, *BH & HPA.*
e-mail: ulwell.farm@virgin.net
website: www.ulwellfarm.co.uk

visit the FHG website www.holidayguides.com

CARAVAN SITES AND NIGHT HALTS

BERE REGIS

🆂 Å See also Colour Display Advertisement

Mr and Mrs R. Cargill, Rowlands Wait Touring Park, Rye Hill, Bere Regis BH20 7LP (01929 472727). Situated in an Area of Outstanding Natural Beauty and overlooking the picturesque village of Bere Regis in the heart of Thomas Hardy country and the beautiful Purbecks. A good base for touring; direct access onto heathland and woodland walks. Ideal for nature lovers, bird watching and quiet family holidays. Park facilities include shop, launderette, gas exchange, children's play area, games room, crazy golf, clean, modern facilities, grassy pitches. Tents also welcome. Dogs welcome.Telephone now for a free colour brochure and details of our special weekend offers. A warm welcome awaits you. **ETC ★★★** *MEMBERS OF THE COUNTRYSIDE DISCOVERY, DAVID BELLAMY GOLD AWARD.* **website: www.rowlandswait.co.uk**

BLANDFORD

🆂 Å See also Colour Display Advertisement

Mr and Mrs W.J. Cooper, "The Inside Park", Down House Estate, Blandford DT11 9AD (01258 453719; Fax: 01258 459921). Situated two miles south-west of Blandford Forum on the Winterborne Stickland road, this is an ideal centre from which to explore Dorset. Offering rural seclusion, yet only minutes from the town; landscaped within established parkland on a 900 acre mixed farm with footpaths through old pleasure gardens, it offers ample space for 120 touring caravans, campers and tents, etc. Within easy reach of Kingston Lacey House, New Forest, Dorchester, Cranborne Chase, Milton Abbas, Corfe Castle and miles of varied coastline. Our facilities include WCs, showers with free hot water housed within our 18th century stable and coach house, full disabled facilities, shop, launderette, electric hook-ups, games room and children's play area, chemical disposal facility, gas, etc. Credit card bookings by telephone welcome. **AA** *THREE PENNANTS*, **RAC** *APPOINTED.* **website: http://members.aol.com/inspark/inspark**

DORCHESTER

🆂 Å

R. and M. Paul, Giant's Head Caravan and Camping Park, Old Sherborne Road, Cerne Abbas, Dorchester (01300 341242). This site is two miles north-east of Cerne Abbas on the Buckland/Newton Road; from Dorchester avoiding bypass; at Top-o'-Town roundabout take Sherborne road, after 500 yards fork right at Loder's Garage, signposted. We are in an ideal position for a motoring, cycling or walking holiday. Places to visit include Cheddar Caves, Longleat House and Lion Reserve, Thomas Hardy's birthplace and various wildlife parks. Fishing, boating and bathing at Weymouth and Portland. Dorchester 8 miles, Sherborne 11. A quiet site with wonderful views of Dorset Downs and the Blackmoor Vale. Site facilities include toilets, water supply, showers. Electric hook-ups available. Laundry room. Hot water. Children welcome, and pets accepted if kept on lead. Good approach road. Site holds 60 caravans and tents; campers and camper vans also welcome. Terms on request. Also available, self-catering. **e-mail: holidays@giantshead.co.uk   website: www.giantshead.co.uk**

The Jurassic Coast
East Devon + Dorset
website: www.jurassiccoast.com
England's first natural World Heritage Site - 95 miles of unspoilt cliffs and beaches, tracing over 185 million years of Earth's history.

Hook Farm Caravan & Camping Park, Gore Lane, Uplyme, Lyme Regis DT7 3UU (01297 442801). Hook Farm nestles in an Area of Outstanding Natural Beauty with breathtaking views of the Lym Valley – peace and tranquillity awaits! As the closest park to Lyme Regis (one mile) it is ideal for both families and walkers. Beach and town facilities are an easy stroll away whilst such stunning walks as the South West Coastal Path and the East Devon Way are on the doorstep. Dorset and Devon's fabulous attractions are within easy reach by car. Camping pitches and static caravans for hire. New toilet block and on-site shop. Dogs welcome. Please call for a brochure. **AA.**
website: www.hookfarm-uplyme.co.uk

POOLE (near)
Merley Court Touring Park, Merley, Wimborne, Near Poole BH21 3AA (01202 881488; Fax: 01202 881484). Widely recognised as one of the finest and most well-equipped touring parks in Britain, Caravan Magazine "Readers' Site of the Year" 2001, AA "Campsite of the Year" 1999, Practical Caravan Magazine "Best Family Park" 1993 and 1997. The facilities at Merley Court are extensive and include shop, take-away food bar, licensed bar (with family room), games room, heated outdoor swimming pool, tennis court, adventure playground, croquet and beautifully landscaped walled garden. Open from 1st March to January 7th. Terms from £10.50 (incl electricity) per night. Touring caravans, tents and motor vans welcome. **ETC ★★★★★**
e-mail: holidays@merley-court.co.uk   website: www.merley-court.co.uk

South Lytchett Manor Caravan Park, Lytchett Minster, Poole BH16 6JB (01202 622577; Fax: 01202 622620) A popular site in lovely rural parkland surroundings. Ideal base for touring Poole Harbour, Bournemouth, Purbecks, Corfe Castle, New Forest. Beautiful beaches at Sandbanks, Studland and Shell Bay. Modern washing facilities, laundry, free hot showers and hairdryers, play area and outdoor table tennis. Facilities for people with disabilities. Well-stocked shop, Calor gas, TV lounge, public telephone. Breakfast Bar in high season. Dogs welcome on lead. Brochure on request. *AA THREE PENNANTS, CARAVAN AND CAMPING CLUB LISTED, B.H. & H.P.A MEMBERS.*
e-mail: slmcp@talk21.com

Wareham Forest Tourist Park, North Trigon, Wareham BH20 7NZ (Tel & Fax: 01929 551393). Enjoy the peace and tranquillity of Wareham Forest, together with the luxury of our park. We offer a choice of fully serviced electric or standard pitches, grass/hard standing Heated outdoor swimming pool and children's paddling pool open all day free (high season); children's adventure playground. Self-service shop/off licence; launderette; washing up room; heated toilet block during winter period; unisex disabled room. Dogs permitted strictly on leads in designated areas. Open all year. Midway between Wareham and Bere Regis, off A35. Credit cards accepted. Resident proprietors: **Tony and Sarah Birch.** Please see our detailed website or call for a brochure. **ETC ★★★★★** *TOURING PARK, DAVID*

BELLAMY SILVER CONSERVATION AWARD.
e-mail: holiday@wareham-forest.co.uk   website: www.wareham-forest.co.uk

---

Abbotsbury Swannery
Near Bridport, Dorset • 01305 871858
Up to 600 free-flying swans – help feed them twice daily. Baby swans hatch May/June.
AV show, coffee shop and gift shop.

Pebble Bank Caravan Park, Camp Road, Wyke Regis, Weymouth DT4 9HF (01305 774844). Pebble Bank Caravan Park is situated one-and-a-half miles from Weymouth town centre. The Park is broadly divided into two sections, one for touring vans/campers and recreational space, the other for privately owned static holiday vans, some of which are let for holiday bookings. Facilities include numerous water points and electric hook-ups, first class toilet and shower facilities and chemical disposal points, laundry room, children's play area, etc. Dogs allowed provided they are well behaved and kept on leads. Our aim is to give the discerning visitor the most relaxed, comfortable and enjoyable holiday possible. Brochure available. **AA** *TWO PENNANTS*

e-mail: info@pebblebank.co.uk

website: www.pebblebank.co.uk

See also Colour Display Advertisement

Woolsbridge Manor Farm Caravan Park, Three Legged Cross, Wimborne BH21 6RA (01202 826369). Situated approximately three-and-a-half-miles from the New Forest market town of Ringwood – easy access to the south coast. Seven acres level, semi-sheltered, well-drained spacious pitches. Quiet country location on a working farm, ideal and safe for families. Showers, mother/baby area, laundry room, washing up area, chemical disposal, payphone, electric hook-ups, battery charging. Children's play area on site. Site shop. Dogs welcome on leads. Fishing adjacent. Moors Valley Country Park golf course one mile. Pub and restaurant 10 minutes' walk. **ETC ★★★, AA** *THREE PENNANTS*.

Mr Colin Church, Whitemead Caravan Park, East Burton Road, Wool BH20 6HG (Tel & Fax: 01929 462241). Peaceful, family-run site set in mature woodland. Clean facilities with free hot showers and hot water. We have two children's play areas, a games room. Our NEW, well stocked, shop is open daily selling groceries, sweets, gas, newspapers and accessories. Takeaway food on site. Monkey World is within walking distance, as are the village pubs, restaurants and shops. The Tank Museum is also close by with Lulworth Cove only five miles away. Excellent walking and cycling all round. Dogs welcome. The perfect base to explore the beautiful county of Dorset.
e-mail: nadinechurch@aol.com
website: www.whitemeadcaravanpark.co.uk

Gloucestershire

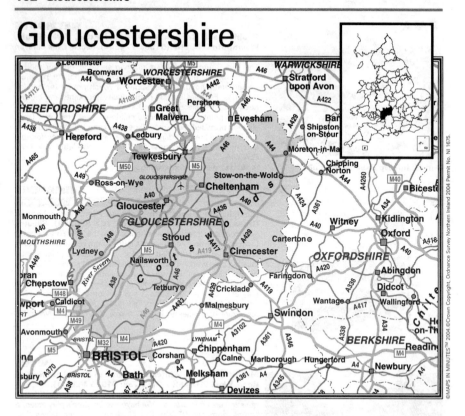

CARAVAN SITES AND NIGHT HALTS

Hogsdown Farm Camp Site, Dursley, Lower Wick GL11 6DB (01453 810224). This site is set between Cotswold Escarpment and Severn Vale in open rural countryside. Many local amenities including swimming, golf, riding, fishing. Tourist attractions include Westonbirt Arboretum, Berkeley Castle, Slimbridge Wild Fowl Trust, Jenner Museum and Cotswold Way. Ideal for touring the many picturesque towns and villages on hills and vales and as a stopover for north/south journeys. Inn within walking distance and many inns and hotels within close proximity. Gas and electric hook-ups available. Laundry, toilets, shower, washing-up facilities. Elsan disposal. Children's play area. Storage available all year. Pets welcome under control. Terms from £7.50 to £9.00 tents, £9.00 caravans and motor homes.

§ Å

Red Lion Inn and Camping and Caravan Park, Wainlode Hill, Norton, Near Gloucester GL2 9LW (Tel & Fax: 01452 730251). Idyllic location in the grounds of a riverside inn in glorious Gloucestershire countryside between the ancient historic city of Gloucester and the famous abbey town of Tewkesbury. Regency Cheltenham Spa and all its attractions lies just a few miles away. We are an ideal base for touring the area with so much to do within easy travelling distance. Interesting walks close by featuring both the Severn and Severn Way Circular and coarse fishing available. You can explore the Forest of Dean, Malvern Hills, the Cotswolds and the Wye Valley. We offer a warm and friendly welcome at all times, and have pitches for touring, tenting and motor caravan users. Facilities include electrical hookups, full toilet and shower facilities, launderette and ironing area and an on-site convenience store. Static caravans also available on-site. **ETC ★★**, *BH & HPA*.
website: www.redlioninn-caravancampingpark.co.uk

§ Å

SLIMBRIDGE

Keith, Joan and Robin Fairall, Tudor Caravan Park, Shepherds Patch, Slimbridge GL2 7BP (01453 890483). Quiet country site next to the Sharpness/Gloucester Canal, 800 yards from the world famous Wildfowl Trust. A David Bellamy Conservation Gold Award Winner since 2000. Ideal base for cycling or touring the Cotswolds. Under the personal supervision of resident owners. Electric hook-ups, hardstandings, toilets, showers, Elsan disposal, separate area for adults only. Visit Berkeley Castle, Gloucester Docks, Bristol, Westonbirt Arboretum, etc. Children and pets welcome. Terms from £9 per night. **AA** *THREE PENNANT SITE*.
e-mail: info@tudorcaravanpark.co.uk
website: www.tudorcaravanpark.co.uk

§

TEWKESBURY

Mill Avon Holiday Park, Gloucester Road, Tewkesbury GL20 5SW (01684 296876). As the name suggests, our Park is bordered on one side by the river Mill Avon and has pleasant views across the Severn Ham to the Malvern Hills. The historic town of Tewkesbury is on the doorstep and a few minutes' walk takes you through picturesque streets past the magnificent 12th century Abbey to the busy shopping centre. The park comprises an area for 24 privately owned holiday caravans and two areas for touring caravans - one accommodates 24 pitches, the other is smaller, accommodating six tourers. All pitches have mains hook-up and awnings are accepted. Modern toilet block, laundry room and chemical toilet point on site. Dogs welcome if kept on lead. Please send for our brochure giving further information and tariffs. Seasonal pitches available .

Please mention the
FHG Guide to Caravan & Camping Holidays
when enquiring about accommodation featured in these pages.

Hampshire

CARAVANS FOR HIRE

HOLIDAY PARKS AND CENTRES

CARAVAN SITES AND NIGHT HALTS

FAREHAM
See also Colour Display Advertisement

Ellerslie Touring Caravan & Camping Park, Downend Road, Fareham PO16 8TS (Tel & Fax: 01329 822248). Only six miles from Continental ferry port. Small, partly wooded site on southern slopes of Portsdown Hill. Next door to riding stables, also health and fitness club, and 600 yards from 27-hole golf course. Within easy reach of excellent boating facilities, also many sites of historic interest. Nicely appointed toilet facilities. Chemical emptying. Food preparation and wash room. Raised barbecues allowed. Free showers. Car and caravan plus two persons, from £8.50 per night. *SOUTHERN TOURIST BOARD GRADED, AA & RAC LISTED, BHHPA.*

GOSPORT
See also Colour Display Advertisement

Kingfisher Caravan Park, Browdown Road, Stokes Bay, Gosport PO13 9BG (023 9250 2611; Fax: 023 9258 3583). The Kingfisher Park is ideal for touring caravans. Only a five minute walk from the beautiful unspoilt Stokes Bay with its breathtaking views of the Solent and Isle of Wight. In addition there are static caravans for hire on individual plots with full services, and holiday homes for sale, new or second hand. On-site facilities include bar, restaurant, shop, launderette, etc. Tourers and motor homes from £13 to £16, Tents from £8 to £16; Caravan Holiday Homes from £125 to £390 per week. Open all year for touring, 10 months for static use - March till 3rd January. **ETC ★★**, *SOUTHERN TOURIST BOARD MEMBER.*

See also Colour Display Advertisement

Hayling Island Family Camp Sites, Hayling Island. Hayling Island is an excellent touring base for Portsmouth, the Isle of Wight, the New Forest, Beaulieu, Chichester, etc. having excellent access to motorways and the Continental ferry port at Portsmouth. Our sites are all family sites, and all are situated near family pubs that cater for children. Hayling Island has safe beaches which have won the Blue Flag for cleanliness many years running. Windsurfing, sailing, horse riding, golf, tennis and walking can be enjoyed here. Heated swimming pool. Long term parking on site - £275 per quarter, including electricity. Please write or telephone for further details to the campsite of your choice. **LOWER TYE CAMPSITE, Copse Lane, Hayling Island PO11 0QB (023 9246 2479); THE OVEN CAMP SITE, Manor Road, Hayling Island PO11 1QX (023 9246 4695).**
e-mail: lowertye@aol.com

website: www.haylingcampsites.co.uk

NEW FOREST

Mrs Jane Pitt, Green Pastures Farm, Ower, Romsey SO51 6AJ (023 8081 4444). A friendly welcome awaits you from Tony and Jane at their family-run farm and campsite. All types of touring units are catered for. Cleanliness is top priority with our toilet facilities, and free hot showers are available. We have a toilet and shower for the disabled; washing machine and dryer; washing-up sinks; electric hook-ups; small shop; Calor and camping gas; payphone. Well-controlled dogs are welcome. Daytime kennels are available. Children love the space, where they can play in full view of the units (parents appreciate that too). 20 minutes' walk to local pub, serving good food. Fishing and golf nearby. **ETC ★★★, AA** *THREE PENNANTS.*
e-mail: enquiries@greenpasturesfarm.com
website: www.greenpasturesfarm.com.

RINGWOOD (near)

Red Shoot Camping Park, Linwood, Near Ringwood BH24 3QT (01425 473789; Fax: 01425 471558). Beautifully situated in the heart of the NEW FOREST, yet only half-an- hour's drive to Bournemouth and coast. Four acres of close mown meadow. Ideal centre for walking and touring and for nature lovers. Pets welcome. Open 1st March to 31st October *Approved site - tents and caravans *Good toilets and showers *Facilities for disabled visitors *Well stocked shop *Safe playground *Mountain bike hire *Laundry room *Electric hook-ups *Forest Inn adjacent - families and dogs welcomed *Owner-managed to high standard. Please send SAE for brochure. From east turn off M27 at Exit 1 and follow signs to Linwood. From west turn off A388 two miles north of Ringwood and look for our sign. **ETC ★★★★**
e-mail: enquiries@redshoot-campingpark.com   website: www.redshoot-campingpark.com

CAMPING SITES

HAYLING ISLAND

See also Colour Display Advertisement

Hayling Island Family Camp Sites, Hayling Island. Hayling Island is an excellent touring base for Portsmouth, the Isle of Wight, the New Forest, Beaulieu, Chichester, etc. having excellent access to motorways and the Continental ferry port at Portsmouth. Our sites are all family sites, and all are situated near family pubs that cater for children. Hayling Island has safe beaches which have won the Blue Flag for cleanliness many years running. Windsurfing, sailing, horse riding, golf, tennis and walking can be enjoyed here. Swimming pool at The Oven campsite. Long term parking on site - £275 per quarter, including electricity. Please write or telephone for further details to the campsite of your choice. **LOWER TYE CAMPSITE, Copse Lane, Hayling Island PO11 0QB (023 9246 2479); THE OVEN CAMP SITE, Manor Road, Hayling Island PO11 1QX (023 9246 4695).**
e-mail: lowertye@aol.com   website: www.haylingcampsites.co.uk

Isle of Wight

HOLIDAY PARKS AND CENTRES

FREE or REDUCED RATE entry to Holiday Visits and Attractions — see our READERS' OFFER VOUCHERS on pages 41-68

🚐 ☼ ⑨ 🛏

BEMBRIDGE
See also Colour Display Advertisement

Whitecliff Bay Holiday Park, Bembridge PO35 5PL. Family-owned and managed, Whitecliff Bay Holiday Park continues to promote great value family holidays on the beautiful Isle of Wight. Open March to October, we can offer self-catering, half board, chalet or caravan, camping and touring caravans, with special theme holidays. Situated in a rural location adjacent to our own secluded, sandy beach, we have an extensive range of facilities for all ages. Brochure request line **01983 872671** or visit our award-winning website.
website: www.whitecliff-bay.com

CARAVAN SITES AND NIGHT HALTS

⑨ 🛏

SHANKLIN

Landguard Camping, Landguard Manor Road, Shanklin PO37 7PH (01983 867028). Landguard Camping is situated between Sandown and Shanklin and is the perfect base from which to enjoy the delights of the Island. This family site offers you quality camping for tents, caravans and motorhomes. The large, outdoor, heated pool is open daily from Spring Bank Holiday until early September. There are 150 level camping pitches each with an electric hook-up. The fully tiled modern toilet block has free hot water to showers, washbasins and sinks. Terms from £11 to £15 (two persons). Ferry packages all season. **ETC ★★★★, RAC** *APPROVED.*
website: www.landguard-camping.co.uk

The Needles Park
Alum Bay, Isle of Wight • 0870 458 0022
website: www.theneedles.co.uk
Breathtaking scenery and a spectacular chair lift to view Needles Rocks and the famous coloured sand cliffs. Make your own unique souvenir; children's rides, shops, refreshments.

PLEASE NOTE

All the information in this book is given in good faith in the belief that it is correct. However, the publishers cannot guarantee the facts given in these pages, neither are they responsible for changes in policy, ownership or terms that may take place after the date of going to press. Readers should always satisfy themselves that the facilities they require are available and that the terms, if quoted, still apply.

Kent

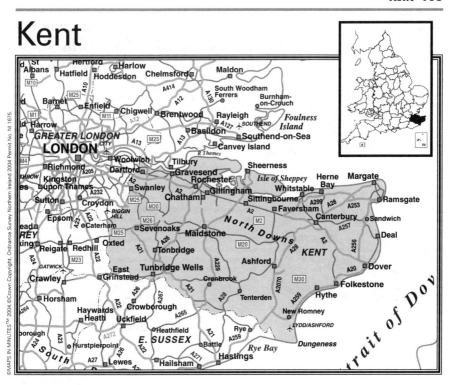

CARAVAN SITES AND NIGHT HALTS

TWO tickets for the price of ONE (cheapest ticket free) at
Museum of Kent Life
see our **READERS' OFFER VOUCHERS** for details

BIRCHINGTON

E.B. Broadley, St Nicholas-at-Wade Camp Site, Court Road, St Nicholas CT7 0NH (01843 847245). Sheltered village site in easy reach of five major towns and seaside. Village (two pubs and post office) signposted off A299 and off A28 near Birchington. Three acres takes 75 units. Open meadow, hedged. Booking advised. Open from 1st March to 31st October. Flush toilets, showers, lighting, shavers. Fishing. Gaz. Touring and motor caravans and tents now welcome, electric hook-ups available. Prices: Tourers £12.50 to £14.50, Motor Caravans £9.50 to £13, Tents £8 to £14. Many places of interest including Ramsgate and Canterbury within easy reach. Birchington is a delightful resort with sand and cliffs.

EASTCHURCH

Warden Springs Holiday Park, Warden Point, Eastchurch, Isle of Sheppey ME12 4HF (01795 880888; Fax: 01795 880218). Directions — M2 turn off Junction 5; A249 to Isle of Sheppey. Turn right at roundabout on Sheppey B2231 to Eastchurch and turn left at church. First right to Warden Point. A secluded park set in a privately owned 38 acre estate surrounded by open farmland and overlooking the sea. On-site amenities include clubhouse with two bars and some live entertainment, shop, showers, toilets, launderette, children's playground, also a great takeaway service and heated outdoor swimming pool. Fishing, boating, and nearby golf. Beautiful cliff top walks and relaxing atmosphere. Booking advisable. From £12.50 to £15.50 per night. Also hire of static carvans. **ETC ★★★**

e-mail: wardensprings@gbholidayparks.co.uk   website: www.gbholidayparks.co.uk

MAIDSTONE

Pine Lodge Touring Park, Ashford Road, Near Bearsted, Maidstone ME17 1XH (01622 730018; Fax: 01622 734498). Pretty, grassed site with woods and fields to side and rear. Large easy access and overnight parking area. 100 pitches and electric hook-ups. Some hard standings. Superb centrally heated shower/toilet block. Hairdryers and shaver points. Laundry and dish washing room. Disabled facilities. Shop for basic needs. Calor Gas exchange. Leeds Castle one mile. Ideal stop for ports, Channel Tunnel and touring Kent. From £10 per night. Sorry, no dogs. Open all year. **ETC ★★★★★**

GUIDE TO SYMBOLS

🚐 **Caravans for Hire**   •   ☼ **Holiday Park/Centre**
🚐 **Caravan Site/Night Halt**   •   ⛺ **Camping Site**

A useful Index of Towns/Villages and Counties appears on page 174 – please also refer to Contents Page 3.

Lancashire

CARAVANS FOR HIRE

LUNE VALLEY
Mrs B Mason, Oxenforth Green, Tatham, Lancaster LA2 8PL (01524 261784). Sleeps 4. Well equipped, modern static caravan on Yorkshire/Lancashire border, four miles from Ingleton. In quiet garden on working farm with panoramic views of Ingleborough and surrounding hills, central for dales, coast and the Lakes. Double and twin beds, TV, shower, fridge, microwave and garden furniture. Terms from £160 per week including gas, electricity and bed linen. Nearest shop one mile, pub three-quarters-of-a mile, and two miles from Bentham 18 hole golf course.

PRESTON

Six Arches Caravan Park, Scorton, Garstang, Near Preston PR3 1AL (01524 791683). Situated on the banks of the River Wyre. Modern caravans and self-catering holiday flats for hire, tourers welcome. Ideally situated for local visitor attractions, Blackpool, Lake District and Trough of Bowland within easy reach. Facilities include outdoor heated pool, club with live entertainment, children's playground and river fishing. Controlled dogs welcome. Telephone for brochure.

HOLIDAY PARKS AND CENTRES

LANCASTER near

Cockerham Sands Country Park, Cockerham, Lancaster LA2 0BB (01524 751387). A family park situated on an inlet to the Irish Sea. Access to 15 miles of the new Lancashire Coastal Walk. Less than an hour to the Lake District, Morecambe or Blackpool. There is a heated swimming pool (June to September), shop, amusement arcade, launderette and the wonderful Cockerham Country Club with live entertainment at weekends. Modern four and six-berth fully equipped caravans for hire plus touring pitches with electric hook-up. Controlled dogs welcome. Write or telephone for brochure.

CARAVAN SITES AND NIGHT HALTS

BLACKPOOL

Mrs Barbara Rawcliffe, Pipers Height Caravan and Camping Park, Peel Road, Peel, Blackpool FY4 5JT (01253 763767). The site is three miles from Blackpool, near A583, and half-mile from M55 - exit Junction 4, turn left, well signed. It accommodates 80 touring caravans and 50 static vans. New static caravan sales. Cottage hire. Booking is advisable in high season. Hot showers, flush toilets, power points, also caravan hard standings and electric hook-up points. Licensed bar and family lounge with entertainment mid and high season, restaurant, games room, launderette. Dogs welcome. Hourly bus service. Facilities available for disabled visitors. Open March to November. Spring time offers. Terms from £14 per night. Strictly families only.

BLACKPOOL

Mrs K. A. Routledge, Gillett Farm Caravan Park Ltd, Peel Road, Peel, Blackpool FY4 5JU (01253 761676). Caravan and camping site three miles from Blackpool, three miles from Lytham and three-and-a-half-miles from St Annes. Only 900 yards from M55 motorway, Exit 4. Turn left onto A583, 400 yards traffic lights turn right and immediately left into Peel Road. Site second on right 350 yards. Golf, fishing and water skiing are available in the area. The site has many amenities including toilets, hot and cold showers, chemical toilet disposal, shaver and hairdryer points, launderette with dryer, ironing room, and public telephone. Camp shop. TV and games room. Mains electric hook-ups. Hard standings. Gas cylinders exchanged. Children welcome. Dogs must be kept on lead. Terms from £7.50 to £14.25.

BLACKPOOL

Mr S. Adams, Stanah House Caravan Park, River Road, Thornton/Cleveleys FY5 5LR (01253 824000; Tel & Fax: 07092 191457). Stanah House Caravan Park is a small, select touring site overlooking the River Wyre and with good views of the Fells and Lake District mountains. Situated nearby is the Wyreside Ecology Centre at the Wyre Estuary Country Park, perfect for a leisurely rural stroll meandering around the banks of the river or the thrill of sailing and water ski-ing with close access to a slipway. In contrast, Blackpool with its varied attractions is easily accessible. The site is of recent construction, with good roads, and has a modern, fully-tiled toilet block with shower rooms and all amenities including laundry room. There is an adventure play area for children. Some sites are available with hard standings and electric hook-ups. There is ample room for caravan and boat storage. Bookings are taken for all periods.
e-mail: stanahhouse@talk21.com

Leicestershire

CARAVAN SITES AND NIGHT HALTS

WOLVEY

Wolvey Caravan Park, Villa Farm, Wolvey, Near Hinckley, LE10 3HF (01455 220493/220630). A quiet site situated on the borders of Warwickshire and Leicestershire, ideally located to explore the many places of interest in the Midlands. Site facilities include shop (licensed), toilets, showers, washrooms, launderette, TV room, 9 hole putting green, fishing. Tents from £7 per night; car, caravan and two persons £7.20 per night (extra person £1); dogs 50p per night; disabled unit, hook-ups £2.25. Tariff and brochure available on request. Registered with the Caravan and Camping Club of Great Britain, **RAC, AA ★★★** www.wolveycaravansite.itgo.com

Lincolnshire

HOLIDAY PARKS AND CENTRES

BOSTON

See also Colour Display Advertisement

Orchard Holiday Park, Frampton Lane, Hubbert's Bridge, Boston PE20 3QU (01205 290328/290368; Fax: 01205 290247). Perfect for fishing, walking, sightseeing, shopping, touring, cycling – or simply relaxing! Nestling quietly in some 36 acres of delightfully landscaped parkland, Orchard Holiday Park is one of Lincolnshire's hidden jewels, where you can be as active or relaxed as you wish. Five-acre fishing lake. First-class amenities and services including licensed bar and new restaurant, shop, launderette, shower blocks etc. 120 luxury Holiday Homes, all with mains electricity, water and drainage. Separate area for touring caravans with mains electricity and water. *DAVID BELLAMY GOLD AWARD.*

CARAVAN SITES AND NIGHT HALTS

BOSTON

Mr & Mrs Lannen, The White Cat Caravan & Camping Park, Shaw Lane, Old Leake, Boston PE22 9LQ (01205 870121). The park of two-and-a-half acres is situated in quiet, rural surroundings and can be found eight miles outside Boston on the A52 Skegness road, turn right opposite the B1184 Sibsey road, the park is 300 yards on the left. Flush toilets, handbasins, H&C, chemical disposal point, free showers, washroom, razor points, electric hook-ups, site shop and children's swings. Dogs allowed. Public houses and restaurants nearby. £9 per night for low season rising to £11 high season. Six, seven and eight-berth caravans for hire from £185 per week. Open April to October. Ideal for touring and local fishing. Further details on request. **AA** *THREE PENNANTS.*

e-mail: kevin@klannen.freeserve.co.uk   website: www.whitecatpark.com

GRANTHAM
See also Colour Display Advertisement

Woodland Waters, Willoughby Road, Ancaster, Grantham NG32 3RT (Tel & Fax: 01400 230888). Set in 72 acres of parkland. Five fishing lakes. Large touring and camping site with electric hook-ups. Luxury holiday lodges. Excellent toilets, shower block with disabled facilities. Bar/restaurant on site. Children's play area. Dogs welcome. Four golf courses nearby. Rallies welcome. Open all year.
e-mail: info@woodlandwaters.co.uk
website: www.woodlandwaters.co.uk

Norfolk

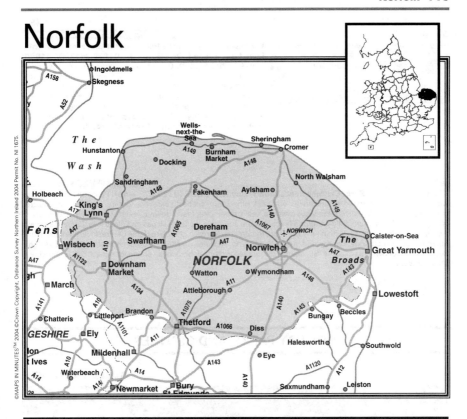

CARAVANS FOR HIRE

DISS

See also Colour Display Advertisement

Waveney Valley Holiday Park, Airstation Farm, Airstation Lane lane, Rushall, Diss IP21 4QF (01379 741228/741690; Fax: 01379 741228). Good access to large, level site two miles east of Dickleburgh, midway between Ipswich and Norwich. Touring caravan and camping park and self-catering stationary caravans. Electric hook-ups; licensed bar, restaurant, shop, laundry, swimming pool. Horse riding; good fishing in locality.
**e-mail: waveneyvalleyholidaypark@compuserve.com
website: www.caravanparksnorfolk.co.uk**

MUNDESLEY-ON-SEA

Kiln Cliffs Caravan Park, Cromer Road, Mundesley NR11 8DF (01263 720449). Peaceful family-run site with NO clubhouse situated around an historic brick kiln. Luxury six-berth caravans for hire, standing on ten acres of grassy cliff top. Magnificent view out over the sea; private path leads down to extensive stretches of unspoilt sandy beach. All caravans fully equipped (except linen) and price includes all gas and electricity. Caravans always available for sale or for hire. Within easy reach are the Broads, Norwich, the Shire Horse Centre, local markets, nature reserves, bird sanctuaries; nearby golf, riding and fishing. Facilities on site include general store and launderette. Responsible pet owners welcome. Substantial discounts for off-peak bookings - phone for details. Call for brochure: **Mr R. Easton.**

HOLIDAY PARKS AND CENTRES

GREAT YARMOUTH

See also Colour Advertisement.

NORWICH

See also Colour Display Advertisement

Golden Beach Holiday Centre, Beach Road, Sea Palling NR12 0AL (01692 598269; Fax: 01692 598693). The Golden Beach Holiday Centre nestles beneath a bank of dunes, beyond which are some of the finest sands in East Anglia. We know just how important your family holiday is for you and and in a luxurious holiday home at the Golden Beach Centre, with its full on-site facilities, relaxation and enjoyment are assured. Luxury holiday homes to rent or for sale; on-site shop; restaurant, bar; launderette; children's play area; shower rooms and toilet facilities; mains electricity. Perfect centre for exploring Norfolk and The Broads. Open March 22nd to October 31st. **ETC ★★★, AA** *THREE PENNANTS, BH & HPA.*

CARAVAN SITES AND NIGHT HALTS

GREAT YARMOUTH

Mrs B.A. Rawnsley, Scratby Hall Caravan Park, Scratby, Great Yarmouth NR29 3PH (01493 730283). Situated on B1159, five miles from the centre of Great Yarmouth, three-quarters-of a mile from the sea and one-and-a-half miles from the Norfolk Broads. Amenities include flush toilets, hot and cold water, free showers, electric hook-ups. Laundry, shop for your needs, games room. Facilities for the disabled. Golf and horse riding nearby. Licences for 108 tourers and tents. Dogs allowed, must be on leads. Open Easter to October. Advance bookings advisable at peak times. A quiet, secluded site, level and grassy. **ETC ★★★★, AA** *THREE PENNANTS*, **RAC.**

MUNDESLEY

Mr Shreeve, Sandy Gulls Caravan Park Ltd., Cromer Road, Mundesley NR11 8DF (01263 720513). A safe cliff top location, miles of clean sandy beaches. The park is gently sloping to ensure good sea views to all visitors. All pitches given plenty of personal space; all-grass pitches, 40 pitches with hook-ups. Suitable for disabled visitors. New hot showers. Shop nearby. Golf (three courses), fishing (sea and fresh water), horse riding close by. Norfolk Broads 10 miles. Great Yarmouth 30 miles, Cromer five miles, Sheringham nine miles and Norwich 24 miles. This park does not cater for children. **ETC ★★★,** *DAVID BELLAMY SILVER AWARD.*

THETFORD

See also Colour Display Advertisement

Lowe Caravan Park, Thetford. Small, friendly country park. Primarily a touring park, we now have four luxury holiday homes for hire in peaceful surroundings. Ideal for touring East Anglia or a quiet relaxing break. More suited to over 50s, but children are welcome. Please contact: **May Lowe, Ashdale, Hills Road, Saham Hills (near Watton), Thetford IP25 7EZ (01953 88105**

Northumberland

The Northumberland map shows towns and roads including Berwick-upon-Tweed, Holy Island, Coldstream, Belford, Galashiels, Kelso, Selkirk, Jedburgh, Hawick, The Cheviot Hills, Alnwick, Rothbury, Amble, Otterburn, Ashington, Newbiggin-by-the-Sea, Morpeth, Bedlington, Blyth, Cramlington, Ponteland, Whitley Bay, Tynemouth, South Shields, Gosforth, NEWCASTLE UPON TYNE, Hexham, Corbridge, Gateshead, Jarrow, TYNE & WEAR, SUNDERLAND, Consett, Washington, Stanley, Houghton le Spring, Chester-le-Street, Peterlee, Durham, Brandon, CUMBRIA, Carlisle, Wigton, Aleton, Brampton, Longtown, Gretna, Annan, Lockerbie, Langholm, BORDERS, The Borders, Peebles, MIDLOTHIAN.

CARAVANS FOR HIRE

BERWICK-UPON-TWEED

Haggerston Castle Holiday Park, Berwick-upon-Tweed. Two and three bedroomed caravans to let, all mod cons - shower, toilet, fridge, microwave and TV. Very popular site. Ideal for a family holiday. Pet friendly available. All amenities on site - clubs, swimming pools, etc. 24 hour security. Close to Scottish Borders, ideal for visiting all popular venues such as Alnwick, Holy Island, Berwick and many more historic sites. **Telephone: 0191 512 1378, 07919 400208 or 07947 314107. website: www.djcaravanholidays.com**

Grace Darling Museum

Bamburgh, Northumberland • 01668 214465

Commemorates the rescue by Grace and her father of the nine survivors of the wreck of the Forfarshire. Many original relics, including the cable used in the rescue, plus books, paintings etc.

CARAVAN SITES AND NIGHT HALTS

ALNWICK

Alnwick Rugby Football Club Ltd (01665 510109). The nine-acre site is located on the southern edge of Alnwick and has a Clubhouse open 24 hours from late April until the end of August. The Clubroom itself is open in the evenings except Mondays and Wednesdays. Alnwick town centre is a fifteen minute walk or a five minute bus ride away. Alnwick is an ancient market town with an imposing castle, the home of the Duke of Northumberland and within the grounds, the magnificently restored Alnwick Garden. The renowned Northumberland Coastline with its castles and sandy beaches is less than fifteen minutes away by car.

BAMBURGH

Glororum Caravan Park, Glororum, Bamburgh NE69 7AW (01668 214457). Beautifully situated one mile from Bamburgh on the glorious Northumberland coast. Set in peaceful surroundings within easy reach of Holy Island, the Farne Islands, the Cheviots and many historic castles. There are ample opportunities locally for swimming, golf, tennis, sailing, water sports, etc. The park facilities include a shop, toilet blocks with showers, laundry with washing machines and drying facilities and children's play area. Please send for our colour brochure and tariff leaflet. **ETC ★★★**
e-mail: info@glororum-caravanpark.co.uk
website: www.glororum-caravanpark.co.uk

CORBRIDGE

Mr K. Richardson, Well House Farm Caravan Park, Corbridge, Stocksfield NE43 7UY (01661 842193). A peaceful site three miles from Corbridge and ten miles from Hexham. Twenty pitches for caravans and tents, with some hardstandings and electric hook-ups. Facilities include toilets, showers etc. Well located for exploring Northumberland and surrounding areas; one mile from the Roman Wall and Hadrian's Wall Path; Newcastle and Metro Centre twelve miles. Terms from £8 per night. **ETC ★★★**

HEXHAM

Causey Hill Caravan Park, Causey Hill, Hexham NE46 2JN (Tel & Fax: 01434 602834). Visit Causey Hill Caravan Park where a warm welcome awaits you. A quiet, family-run park offering high standard facilities set in secluded picturesque countryside. Large natural pond features, sheltered woodland walks, stunning views. Situated one and a half miles south west of Hexham; five miles from Hadrian's Wall; 20 miles Metro Shopping Centre. Causey Hill provides holiday homes and pitches for sale; touring pitches, some hard standings from £12; camping pitches from £9. Electric hook-ups. Directions: Hexham town centre at Yellow Box Junction turn onto B6306, first right signed Hexham Racecourse one and a half miles, crossroads right again, first right 200 metres on left. **ETC/AA/RAC ★★★**, *BRITISH GRADED HOLIDAY PARK.*
e-mail: causeyhill@aol.com

CAMPING SITES

HEXHAM

Mr & Mrs D Maughan, Greencarts Farm, Humshaugh, Hexham NE46 4BW (01434 681320; mobile: 07752 697355). Greencarts is a working farm situated in Roman Wall country, ideally placed for exploring by car, bike or walking. It has magnificent views of the Tyne Valley. Convenient for Hexham Racecourse. Fishing available locally. Campsite, for 30 tents and bunk barn with 12 beds, showers and toilets are now open from Easter to the end of October. Prices for campsite are £5 to £10 per tent plus £1 per person, bunk barn beds from £10, linen available. All welcome. En suite Bed and Breakfast accommodation available all year in our farmhouse, from £25 to £35.
e-mail: sandra@greencarts.co.uk

Nottinghamshire

CARAVAN SITES AND NIGHT HALTS

TUXFORD

Orchard Park Touring Caravan and Camping Park, Marnham Road, Tuxford NG22 0PY (01777 870228, Fax: 01777 870320). Quiet, sheltered Park set in an old orchard. Ideal for Sherwood Forest and many attractions, all pitches with electric hook-up, separate games field, dog walk, excellent heated facilities with free hot showers and facilities for disabled. Brochure available on request. **AA** *THREE PENNANTS.*
website: www.orchardcaravanpark.co.uk

TUXFORD
See also Colour Display Advertisement

Steve and Martin Bailey, Greenacres Caravan & Touring Park, Lincoln Road, Tuxford NG22 0JN (Tel & Fax: 01777 870264). Greenacres is a family-run holiday park in north Nottinghamshire often referred to as "a gem set in the heart of Robin Hood country". Facilities offered include electric hook-ups, laundry, dishwashing and vegetable preparation area, good clean toilet block incorporating showers, wcs etc, children's play area with swings and slide, separate recreational field, shop, telephone, tourist information centre. Calor gas and camping Gaz available on site. The park is ideal as both an overnight halt or a base for exploring the surrounding countryside. Static caravans for sale and hire. Directions: A1(S) Leave at 'Tuxford local services' sign. At T-junction turn right (sp Lincoln A57), follow brown signs, Fountain Pub on left, site 50 yards on left. A1(N) Leave at 'Tuxford' sign. At village centre turn right, follow road under A1 bridge, follow brown signs, Fountain Pub on left, site 50 yards on left. *BH & HPA MEMBER.*
e-mail: bailey-security@freezone.co.uk   website: http://members.freezone.co.uk/bailey-security/

Shropshire

CARAVAN SITES AND NIGHT HALTS

TELFORD

Severn Gorge Park, Bridgnorth Road, Tweedale, Telford TF7 4JB (Tel & Fax: 01952 684789). Set amongst woodland, this level and sheltered site provides a perfect base for exploring Ironbridge Gorge, Museums, Cosford Aerospace Museum, Severn Valley Railway, Bridgnorth, Shrewsbury, Much Wenlock. Site facilities include reception/shop, centrally heated toilet and shower block, washing up sinks, laundry, disabled shower and toilet, baby change and bath, children's play area, public telephone, dog exercise area, electric hook-ups, hard standings. Open all year. Please write or phone for FREE brochure. **ETC ★★★★★, AA/RAC** *LISTED*
e-mail: info@severngorgepark.co.uk
website: www.severngorgepark.co.uk

ENGLAND Ratings You Can Trust

The English Tourism Council (formerly the English Tourist Board) has joined with the **AA** and **RAC** to create a new, easily understood quality rating for serviced accommodation, giving a clear guide of what to expect.

HOTELS are given a rating from One to Five **Stars.**

GUEST ACCOMMODATION, which includes guest houses, bed and breakfasts, inns and farmhouses, is rated from One to Five **Diamonds**.

HOLIDAY PARKS, TOURING PARKS and CAMPING PARKS – standards of quality range from a One Star (acceptable) to a Five Star (exceptional) park.

SELF-CATERING – the more **Stars** (from One to Five) awarded to an establishment, the higher the levels of quality you can expect. Establishments at higher rating levels also have to meet some additional requirements for facilities.

SCOTLAND

Star Quality Grades will reflect the most important aspects of a visit, such as the warmth of welcome, efficiency and friendliness of service, the quality of the food and the cleanliness and condition of the furnishings, fittings and decor.

THE MORE STARS, THE HIGHER THE STANDARDS.

The description, such as Hotel, Guest House, Bed and Breakfast, Lodge, Holiday Park, Self-catering etc tells you the type of property and style of operation.

WALES

STAR QUALITY GUIDE FOR

HOTELS, GUEST HOUSES AND FARMHOUSES

SELF-CATERING ACCOMMODATION (Cottages, Apartments, Houses)

CARAVAN HOLIDAY HOME PARKS (Holiday Parks, Touring Parks, Camping Parks)

Places which score highly will have an especially welcoming atmosphere and pleasing ambience, high levels of comfort and guest care, and attractive surroundings enhanced by thoughtful design and attention to detail.

Somerset

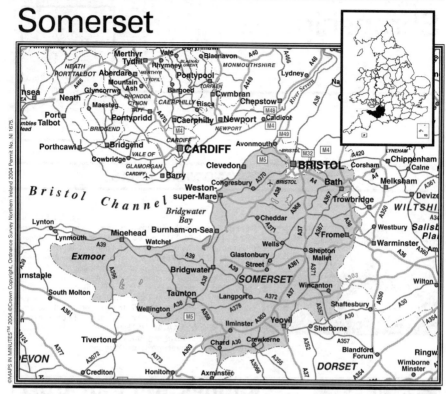

CARAVANS FOR HIRE

DULVERTON

Mrs M.M. Jones, Higher Town, Dulverton TA22 9RX (01398 341272). Our farm is situated half-a-mile from open moorland, one mile from the Devon/Somerset border and four miles from Dulverton. 80 acres of the farm is in the Exmoor National Park. We let two caravans which are quarter-of-a-mile apart and do not overlook each other, and have lovely views, situated in lawns with parking space. Both are 8-berth, with a double end bedroom, bunk bedroom, shower, flush toilet, hot/cold water and colour TV. The caravans are modern and fully equipped except linen. Cot and high chair available. One caravan with three bedrooms. Visitors are welcome to watch the milking or walk over our beef and sheep farm. Riding and fishing nearby. Open May to October. Price from £120, includes gas and electricity.

WOOKEY HOLE

Mrs E.A. Gibbs, Ebborlands Farm & Riding Centre, Wookey Hole, Wells BA5 1AY (Tel & Fax: 01749 672550). Sleeps 6. Six-berth luxury caravan. Two separate bedrooms, bathroom with toilet/shower/washbasin, bedroom/lounge, kitchen. Own private site situated on the southern slopes of the Mendip Hills, a few minutes' walk from Wookey Hole village, but away from the main traffic route to the caves. Two-and-a-half miles from the city of Wells. Good touring area for Somerset, surrounding counties and Severn crossings into Wales. Lots of country footpaths - near West Mendip Way, Ebbor Gorge and surrounding hills. Horse riding available from our centre nearby. Rates from £100 to £250 per week according to season.
e-mail: EileenG@btinternet.com

HOLIDAY PARKS AND CENTRES

CHEDDAR

Taste The Real Cheddar!

at **BROADWAY HOUSE**

Holiday Touring Caravan & Camping Park

HOLIDAY CARAVANS FOR HIRE
PREMIER TOURING AND CAMPING PITCHES
FREE HEATED SWIMMING POOL
FREE MARVELOUS ADVENTURE PLAYGROUND/PIXIE AREA
DISABLED AND BABIES ROOM
CORNER SHOP WITH THE FRIENDLY SERVICE
COME AND SEE OUR PET LLAMA AND PARROT

FREE ENTRANCE TO "ENGLISH PUB" & FAMILY ROOM
BARBEQUES FOR YOUR OWN USE
LAUNDERETTE, SUNBED, AMUSEMENTS, CRAZY GOLF, BOULES,
SKATEBOARD PARK, INDOOR TABLE TENNIS
BMX TRACK, CYCLE HIRE
ACTIVITY PROGRAMME
ARCHERY, RIFLE SHOOTING,
ABSEILING, CAVING, CANOEING, NATURE TRAILS.

BROADWAY HOUSE CHEDDAR SOMERSET. BS27 3DB
TEL:01934 742610 FAX:01934 744950
email: enquiries@broadwayhouse.uk.com www.broadwayhouse.uk.com

MINEHEAD

See also Colour Display Advertisement

St Audries Bay Holiday Club, West Quantoxhead, near Minehead TA4 4DY (01984 632515; Fax: 01984 632785). Award-winning park on the Somerset coast, with splendid views and beach access. Indoor heated pool, family entertainment in school holidays, wide range of sports and leisure facilities, licensed bar and restaurant, all- day snack bar and takeaway. Situated 15 miles from the M5, near Exmoor at the foot of the Quantock Hills. Well-maintained level site. On-site shop. Family-owned and managed. Half board holidays available in comfortable chalets, self-catering in luxury caravans. Touring caravans and tents welcome. Luxury holiday homes for sale. **ETC ★★★★,** *BHHPA DAVID BELLAMY GOLD AWARD.*
e-mail: mrandle@staudriesbay.co.uk
website: www.staudriesbay.co.uk

One child FREE with two full-paying adults at
The Helicopter Museum
see our **READERS' OFFER VOUCHERS** for details

TAUNTON
See also Colour Display Advertisement

Michael & Sarah Barrett, Quantock Orchard Caravan Park, Flaxpool, Crowcombe, Near Taunton TA4 4AW (01984 618618). A small family-run touring park set in the beautiful Quantock Hills close to Exmoor and the coast in a designated Area of Outstanding Natural Beauty - we look forward to welcoming you to our five star park at any time of the year. Please phone or write for colour brochure and tariff. **ETC** ★★★★★, **AA** *FOUR PENNANTS, DELUXE PARK*
e-mail: qocp@flaxpool.freeserve.co.uk
website: www.quantockorchard.co.uk

CARAVAN SITES AND NIGHT HALTS

BATH
See also Colour Display Advertisement

Newton Mill Camping Park, Newton Road, Bath BA2 9JF. (01225 333909). Proprietors: **Keith and Louise Davies.** OPEN ALL YEAR, Newton Mill Camping Park lies in an idyllically beautiful valley VERY CLOSE TO THE CENTRE OF BATH, to which it is connected by a nearby very frequent bus service and the level, traffic-free Bristol-Bath cycle path. We have a well stocked shop, a restaurant serving a range of reasonably priced meals and our Old Mill Bar lying beside the millstream. There are separate level tent meadows and caravan pitches and all roads are tarmac. The amenity blocks are of a very high standard and include bathrooms and other private rooms. Directions: on the A4 to the west of Bath, take the exit signposted Newton St Loe at the roundabout by the Globe Inn. Park is one mile on the left. **ETC** ★★★★, **AA** *FOUR PENNANTS, DAVID BELLAMY GOLD CONSERVATION AWARD.*
e-mail: newtonmill@hotmail.com
website: www.campinginbath.co.uk

BRIDGWATER

Mill Farm Caravan and Camping Park, Fiddington, Bridgwater TA5 1JQ. Attractive, sheltered farm site situated between beautiful Quantock Hills and the sea. Boating, swings, table tennis, TV, tourist information and large sand pit. Tropical indoor heated pool and two outdoor pools with giant waterslide. Canoes, trampolines and ponies for hire. Caravan storage available. Clean toilets, etc. Laundry room, electric hook-ups, camp shop, good local pubs, evening entertainment. Open all year. SELF CATERING HOLIDAY COTTAGE ALSO AVAILABLE. Please write or telephone for brochure. Contact: **M.J. Evans (01278 732286).**
website: www.mill-farm-uk.com

MARTOCK

Mr and Mrs M.A. Broadley, Southfork Caravan Park, Parrett Works, Martock TA12 6AE (01935 825661; Fax: 01935 825122). Small, peaceful, "Excellent" graded touring park in open countryside close to River Parrett. Level, grassy site with clean modern heated toilet block and laundry room and free hot showers. Play area, grocery shop and off-licence, caravan spares and accessories shop. Approved caravan servicing and repair centre. Numerous places of interest nearby for all age groups, an ideal base for touring this lovely part of the West Country. 25 touring pitches, electrical hook-ups, three static holiday caravans for hire. Open all year. For further details please contact **Mr & Mrs M.A. Broadley.** ETC ★★★★, *MEMBER OF SOUTH WEST TOURISM.* BH&HPA.
e-mail: southforkcaravans@btconnect.com

TAUNTON

Mr & Mrs D.A. Small, Ashe Farm Caravan and Camping Site, Thornfalcon, Taunton TA3 5NW (01823 442567; Fax: 01823 443372). In the vale of Taunton Deane, quiet farm site, with 30 touring pitches and two holiday caravans. Sheltered mowed meadow with easy access quarter-mile off A358, four miles south east of Taunton. Showers, toilet, hot water, deep sinks, shaver points, disabled facilities, electric hook-ups, games room and tennis court, laundry. Pets welcome. Ideal touring site within easy reach of North and South coasts and Quantock and Blackdown Hills, Exmoor and the Somerset Levels. The fully equipped holiday caravans sleep six. Open April to October, from £4.25 per person. From M5 Junction 25, take A358 for two and a half miles, then turn right at "Nags Head". ETC ★★★, **AA** *THREE PENNANTS.*

A useful Index of Towns/Villages and Counties appears on page 174 – please also refer to Contents Page 3.

• • *Some Useful Guidance for Guests and Hosts* • •

Every year literally thousands of holidays, short breaks and overnight stops are arranged through our guides, the vast majority without any problems at all. In a handful of cases, however, difficulties do arise about bookings, which often could have been prevented from the outset.

It is important to remember that when accommodation has been booked, both parties – guests and hosts – have entered into a form of contract. We hope that the following points will provide helpful guidance.

GUESTS:
* When enquiring about accommodation, be as precise as possible. Give exact dates, numbers in your party and the ages of any children.
* State the number and type of rooms wanted and also what catering you require – bed and breakfast, full board etc. Make sure that the position about evening meals is clear – and about pets, reductions for children or any other special points.
* Read our reviews carefully to ensure that the proprietors you are going to contact can supply what you want. Ask for a letter confirming all arrangements, if possible.
* If you have to cancel, do so as soon as possible. Proprietors do have the right to retain deposits and under certain circumstances to charge for cancelled holidays if adequate notice is not given and they cannot re-let the accommodation.

HOSTS:
* Give details about your facilities and about any special conditions. Explain your deposit system clearly and arrangements for cancellations, charges etc. and whether or not your terms include VAT.
* If for any reason you are unable to fulfil an agreed booking without adequate notice, you may be under an obligation to arrange suitable alternative accommodation or to make some form of compensation.

While every effort is made to ensure accuracy, we regret that FHG Publications cannot accept responsibility for errors, omissions or misrepresentations in our entries or any consequences thereof. Prices in particular should be checked because we go to press early. We will follow up complaints but cannot act as arbiters or agents for either party.

Staffordshire

CARAVAN SITES AND NIGHT HALTS

COTTON

Star Caravan and Camping Park, Cotton, Near Alton Towers, Stoke-on-Trent ST10 3DW • 01538 702219

Situated off the B5417 road, between Leek and Cheadle, within 10 miles of the market towns of Ashbourne and Uttoxeter, with Alton Towers just one and a quarter miles away. A family-run site where your enjoyment is our main concern. Site amenities include large children's play area, toilet block with free showers, etc., laundry room with drying and ironing facilities, electric hook-ups, etc. Full disabled toilet and shower. Dogs welcome but must be kept on leash. Open 26th March to 1st November. £10 per night for two persons. Modern static caravan and luxury disabled adapted caravan for hire. Brochure and further details available.

website: www.starcaravanpark.co.uk

See also Colour Advertisement

Suffolk

HOLIDAY PARKS AND CENTRES

CAMPING SITES

SUDBURY

Mrs A. Wilson, Willowmere Camping Park, Bures Road, Sudbury CO10 0NN (Tel & Fax: 01787 375559). This neat little site could be suitable for a weekend or as a touring base for inland Suffolk. It has just 40 pitches, 24 with electric points. Site has single toilet block of good quality and well maintained, with free hot water in the washbasins and showers. No other on-site amenities apart from milk, cold drinks etc. Village shops half-a-mile away. Open Easter to October. Terms per unit with two persons from £9. **ETC ★★★**, *BH&HPA*.

Sussex

East Sussex

HOLIDAY PARKS AND CENTRES

☼ **⑤**

ShearBarn Holiday Park, Barely Lane, Hastings TN35 5DX (01424 423583; Fax: 01424 718740). ShearBarn Holiday Park is the family holiday that has it all – countryside and seaside, quiet walks and rural charm, with breathtaking views and modern facilities. ShearBarn puts comfort into camping and caravanning, but those looking for luxury can buy a holiday home at this exclusive park. In the heart of Sussex above the historic resort of Hastings is everything you need for the perfect holiday, with a safe environment for the whole family. Children can enjoy the playgrounds and amusements, with a friendly bar for all the family to relax in.
e-mail: shearbarn@haulfryn.co.uk
website: www.shearbarn.co.uk

P.J. Turner, Badgers Run, 2c The Old Brewery, High Street, Hastings TN34 3ER (01424 712082; Fax: 01424 428018). Four to eight-berth caravans privately owned on a delightful site in Coghurst Hall Holiday Village in over 47 acres of breathtaking scenery and woodlands. The central feature of this picturesque park is a large tree-fringed lake which is regularly used by holiday residents for fishing. The original manor house has been converted into the recently refurbished 'Country Club' with regular family entertainment, as well as housing an adult quiet bar, function room, small amusement arcade and indoor leisure complex with pool, sauna, jacuzzi etc.
e-mail: badgers.run@talk21.com
website: http://badgersrun.thenetzone.co.uk

CARAVAN SITES AND NIGHT HALTS

e-mail: info@crazylane.co.uk

BATTLE
Crazy Lane Touring Park, Whydown Farm, Sedlescombe, Battle TN33 0QT (01424 870147). A small secluded family park situated in a sun trap valley in the heart of 1066 country, within easy reach of beaches and all historical sites. Sailing, horse riding, golf, tennis and fishing facilities are all in easy reach. First class luxury toilet facilities; launderette. All pitches individually numbered. 36 touring, 20 motor caravan, 36 electrical hook-up points. Hardstanding for disabled with own fully equipped toilet facility. Dogs are welcome on lead. Open 1st March to 31st October. From £9.50 per night; book seven nights, only pay for six! Directions - travelling south of A21 turn left 100 yards past Junction B2244 opposite Blackbrooks Garden Centre, into Crazy Lane, site 70 yards on right. ETC ★★★
website: www.crazylane.co.uk

BODIAM
Mr Richard Bailey, Park Farm Caravan and Camping Site, Park Farm, Bodiam TN32 5XA (01580 830514; Fax: 01580 830519). Quiet rural site in beautiful setting. Off B2244, signposted. Hot showers; children's play area. Barbecues permitted. Riverside walk to Bodiam Castle. Free fishing in River Rother. Open Easter to October. Dogs allowed. Charges: £1 per child, £10 per night two adults with caravan or large tent, £5 per person ridge tent. Undercover winter storage available at £6 per week

West Sussex

CARAVAN SITES AND NIGHT HALTS

⑤ Å **ARUNDEL**
Maynard's Caravan and Camping Park, Crossbush, Arundel BN18 9PQ (01903 882075; Fax: 01903 885547). From Arundel on A27 to Worthing, Brighton turn left into car park behind Crossbush Out and Out Restaurant and Pub, three-quarters of a mile, signposted from Arundel. Open all year. £9.00 for two persons including unit, car and hot showers. Electric hook-ups, telephone, children's play area on site. Restaurant and pub adjacent site. Dogs by arrangement. Places to visit include Arundel Castle and Wildfowl Reserve, Littlehampton beach, Sussex Downs and Goodwood Racecourse. Leisure pursuits in the area include sailing, fishing, golf, etc. **RAC**, *BH&HPA, CARAVAN AND CAMPING CLUB.*

⑤ **CHICHESTER**

Bell Caravan Park, Bell Lane, Birdham PO20 7HY (01243 512264). Holiday home (owner-occupied only) and small touring park with electric hook-ups, toilet blocks with showers. Children and dogs welcome. Local shop within walking distance. We are approximately within one/two miles from the beach and Chichester Harbour and Marina are a short drive away. The Roman city of Chichester is about five miles away and there are many places to visit in the area including Goodwood House and racecourse, Petworth House and Arundel Castle. Chichester is also ideal for visiting the historic town of Portsmouth. For prices please telephone or send a SAE.

⑤ Å **HORSHAM near (Dial Post)**

Honeybridge Park, Honeybridge Lane, Dial Post RH13 8NX (Tel & Fax: 01403 710923). Delightfully situated 15 acre park in an Area of Outstanding Natural Beauty. Rural, relaxed atmosphere, highest standards maintained and with generous sized hard standing and grass pitches. Heated amenity blocks with excellent facilities (inc. disabled), licensed shop, take-away, games room and play area. Seasonal pitches and storage facilities available. Ideal touring base convenient to Brighton, Chichester and ports. Only one hour from London and Theme Parks. Ten miles south of Horsham on A24 turn at Old Barn Nurseries. Dogs welcome. Open all year. **ETC ★★★★, AA** *FOUR PENNANTS.* **e-mail: enquiries@honeybridgepark.co.uk website: www.honeybridgepark.co.uk**

Arundel Castle
Arundel, West Sussex • 01903 883136
website: www.arundelcastle.org
The family home of the Dukes of Norfolk for over 850 years. Superb collection of paintings, furniture and armour; restored Victorian kitchen; grounds with chapel.

Weald & Downland Open Air Musem
Chichester, West Sussex • 01243 811348
website: www.wealddown.co.uk
Over 40 historic buildings carefully re-constructed, including medieval farmstead, working flour mill, and Victorian rural school.

Warner Farm, Selsey (01243 604499). Unbeatable prices, fantastic value – touring holiday family fun. Excellent facilities for our visitors include free modern showers and toilets, BBQs, dog walking and children's play areas, with a choice of standard, electric and super pitches. Enjoy all the activities and live entertainment within the other parks, including the fabulous new multi-million pound Oasis Pools and Fitness Centre. Come and try our Five-Star Touring Park in Selsey. Call the hotline for a free brochure or to book. **ETC ★★★★★**
e-mail: touring@bunnleisure.co.uk
website: www.bunnleisure.co.uk

CAMPING SITES

CHICHESTER

Wicks Farm Camping Park, Redlands Lane, West Wittering, Chichester PO20 8QD (01243 513116). Camping Park for tents and motor caravans. Peaceful, rural site with modern toilets, showers and laundry room, with a number of "Electric Pitches". Situated just off the B2179, one mile from the sandy beach of West Wittering, one mile from Chichester harbour at Itchenor. The park is ideally placed for a coastal holiday but within easy reach of many places of interest, including Chichester, Portsmouth and the South Downs. Children and pets welcome. **ETC ★★★★★, AA/RAC** LISTED. DAVID BELLAMY GOLD AWARD.

Tyne & Wear

CARAVAN SITES AND NIGHT HALTS

HAMSTERLEY

Byreside Caravan Site, Hamsterley, Newcastle-upon-Tyne NE17 7RT (01207 560280). The caravan site is on the family-run farm in the beautiful countryside of the Derwent Valley. The site is open all year round and is quiet and secluded. It is very popular with walkers and cyclists as it is adjacent to the Derwent Walk Country Park which is also part of the Coast to Coast route. History looms large in the district with many places to visit in the surrounding area and only a short distance from both Durham and Northumberland. On site is a small shop and toilet block. All pitches have electric hook-up points. Camping area and playing field. Booking advisable. **ETC ★★★★**. Contact: **Mrs J. Clemitson.**

Warwickshire

CARAVAN SITES AND NIGHT HALTS

STRATFORD-UPON-AVON

Dodwell Park, Evesham Road (B439), Stratford-upon-Avon CV37 9SR (01789 204957). A small touring park, very clean and quiet, set in the countryside two miles south west of Stratford-upon-Avon. An ideal location from which to visit Shakespeare's birthplace, Anne Hathaway's Cottage, Warwick Castle and the Cotswolds. The park has a well-provisioned shop with off-licence and gas supplies and plenty of 16 amp hook-ups. There are country walks to the River Avon and the village of Luddington. From Stratford-upon-Avon take B439 (formerly A439) towards Bidford-on-Avon for two miles. The park lies on the left, signposted. Open all year. Rates from £12.50 to £14.00 including electricity. Free brochure on request. **ETC ★★★**

e-mail: enquiries@dodwellpark.co.uk   website: www.dodwellpark.co.uk

Yorkshire

East Yorkshire

HOLIDAY PARKS AND CENTRES

North Yorkshire

CARAVANS FOR HIRE

HARROGATE (near)

The Yorkshire Hussar Inn Holiday Park, Markington, near Harrogate HG3 3NR (01765 677327). Secluded family site nestling deep in the heart of picturesque Yorkshire, midway between Ripon and Harrogate, which is noted for its splendid flower gardens and shops. The park is situated behind the 'olde worlde' inn, in a peaceful garden setting, and is licensed for 75 caravans, plus space for some tourers and tents. There are five luxury six-berth caravans for hire on a weekly basis; nightly lets allowed if available. Each caravan has a double and a twin bedroom, plus sofa bed in the lounge; bathroom/shower room. The caravans are connected to all services, and TV, cooking utensils, crockery, cutlery, duvets and pillows are supplied. Guests must supply own bed linen and towels. Children's play area. Village shop and Post Office. Further details on request from **Mrs Denton.** AA *THREE PENNANTS, BH & HPA.*
e-mail: yorkshirehussar@yahoo.co.uk

ROBIN HOOD'S BAY

Mr and Mrs Hodgson, Low Farm, Robin Hood's Bay YO22 4QF (01947 880366). Spend a lovely holiday in the unique location where the North York Moors roll down to the sea. Our working farm is situated in a pleasant green valley with superb views of rolling countryside and woodland. We can offer you the choice of two well equipped, comfortable, modern caravans with all facilities, one with three bedrooms and one with two. Each is set in its own garden area with picnic table and chairs, and barbecue area. Short breaks available early and late season.
e-mail: hodgson@lowfarm2306.freeserve.co.uk
website: www.lowfarm-rhb.co.uk

e-mail: tony@harmonylodge.net

SCARBOROUGH

Sue and Tony Hewitt, Harmony Country Lodge, Limestone Road, Burniston, Scarborough YO13 0DG (0800 2985840). Set in two acres of private land overlooking the National Park and sea. An ideal base for walking or touring in the beautiful North Yorkshire countryside. TWO miles from Scarborough and within easy reach of many nearby attractions and amenities. Spacious five-berth, fully fitted static caravan with two bedrooms. Shower room with hand basin, hot and cold water, and flush toilet. Fully equipped kitchen, gas cooker and microwave, controlled electric heating and colour TV. Pillows, quilts and linen provided. Picnic table and lawned area. From £100 to £315 per week, gas/electricity included. Parking. B&B available.

website: www.harmonylodge.net

SCARBOROUGH

Mrs M. Edmondson, Plane Tree Cottage Farm, Staintondale, Scarborough YO13 0EY (01723 870796). This small mixed farm is situated off the beaten track, with open views of beautiful countryside and the sea. Large static caravan to let on private site near farm cottage. Lounge with TV, double and twin bedroom and bathroom. Staintondale is about half-way between Scarborough and Whitby and near the North York Moors. An ideal holiday for anyone wanting peace and quiet. Within easy reach of North York Moors Railway, Goathland, Whitby and York. Car essential. Bed and Breakfast also available. More details available on request.

HOLIDAY PARKS AND CENTRES

CONEYSTHORPE

Castle Howard Lakeside Holiday Park, Coneysthorpe, York YO60 7DD (Tel & Fax: 01653 648316). Approved site on private estate, 15 miles north east of York, off A64. The site is within walking distance and with views of Castle Howard, adjacent to the Great Lake. Accommodation for 30 tourers and 30 tents, some serviced sites available. Amenities include hot and cold water, showers; site shop, Calor gas available. Children welcome. Dogs allowed under strict control. Open March to October. Fees on application.

HARROGATE
See also Colour Display Advertisement

Ripley Caravan Park, Ripley, Harrogate HG3 3AU (01423 770050). Situated adjacent to the delightfully quiet village of Ripley, dominated by its castle which has been occupied by the same family for over 600 years. Conveniently placed for the superb holiday and conference town of Harrogate and for historic Knaresborough; an ideal touring base with the Yorkshire Dales close by. The site facilities include a leisure block with games room with colour TV, nursery playroom, telephone, shop and heated indoor swimming pool and sauna; toilet block with showers, ample washbasins, razor points and baby bath. There is a room for our disabled guests with its own specialised facilities. Laundry room, chemical toilet disposal. Electric hook-up points and hard standing for some pitches. Pets welcome by arrangement. Brochure and tariff available on request. ETC ★★★★★, AA *FIVE PENNANTS, DAVID BELLAMY GOLD AWARD*.

☼ ▣ 🚐 Å

WHITBY

Middlewood Farm Holiday Park, Robin Hood's Bay, Near Whitby YO22 4UF (01947 880414; Fax: 01947 880871). Small', peaceful, family park. A walkers', artists' and wildlife paradise, set amidst the beautiful North Yorkshire Moors National Park, Heritage Coast and 'Heartbeat Country'. Relax and enjoy the magnificent panoramic views of our spectacular countryside. Five minutes' walk to the village PUB and shops. Ten minutes' walk to the BEACH and picturesque Robin Hood's Bay. SUPERIOR LUXURY HOLIDAY HOMES FOR HIRE, equipped to the highest standards (1 March - 4 January). TOURERS and TENTS: level, sheltered park with electric hook-ups. Superb heated facilities, free showers and dishwashing. Laundry. Gas. Children's adventure playground. Adjacent dog walk and cycle route. Credit cards accepted. Signposted. A warm welcome awaits you. **ETC★★★★★** *HOLIDAY PARK, ROSE AWARD, WELCOME HOST,* **AA** *THREE PENNANTS, DAVID BELLAMY GOLD AWARD*
e-mail: info@middlewoodfarm.com   **website: www.middlewoodfarm.com**

CARAVAN SITES AND NIGHT HALTS

Å ▣

HUTTON LE HOLE

Hutton Le Hole Caravan Park. A family-run 22-pitch site at Westfield Lodge Farm, on the southern edge of the North Yorkshire Moors. A level, free-draining and secluded site with modern facilities in a picturesque and peaceful location just outside the village of Hutton Le Hole. This site has on-farm walks and is ideal for walking the North York Moors and touring the area. York is one hour's drive and Scarborough and the coast 45 minutes. Castle Howard is 20 minutes' drive away. Open Easter to 31st October. Prices from £10 per night. Enquiries/brochure: **Mrs Annabel Strickland, Westfield Lodge, Hutton Le Hole, York YO62 6UG (01751 417261; Fax: 01751 417876).**
e-mail: rwstrickland@farmersweekly.net
website: www.westfieldlodge.co.uk

🚐

MASHAM

Blackswan Holiday Park, Rear Black Swan, Fearby, Masham, Ripon HG4 4NF (01765 689477). A small family-run park in an Area of Outstanding Natural Beauty, designated by the Countryside Commission. Ideal for walking, six miles from Lightwater Valley Theme Park, two miles from Masham, famous for its two breweries - Theakstons and Blacksheep, both of which have visitor centres. Pub on site serving food and a first class restaurant. Luxury caravans for hire, an ideal place for that quiet, relaxing family holiday. **ETC ★★★**, **AA** *TWO PENNANTS.*
e-mail: info@blackswanholiday.co.uk
website: www.blackswanholiday.co.uk

▣

SCARBOROUGH

Mrs Carol Croft, Cayton Village Caravan Park Ltd, Mill Lane, Cayton Bay, Scarborough YO11 3NN. Situated three miles south of Scarborough, four miles from Filey, half a mile from sandy beach at Cayton Bay. Attractive, sheltered, level, landscaped park adjoining Cayton Village Church with footpath 150 yards to two village inns, fish and chip shop and bus service. Luxurious shower, toilet, disabled toilet, dishwashing and laundry facilities. Central heating plus SUPER SAVER and OAP weeks for low season bookings. Four acre floodlit dog walk, children's adventure playground. Seasonal pitches available Easter to October. Separate rally field. Min/Max touring caravans and tents £9 to £17. £2 awnings, £1 dogs. **Telephone: 01723 583171** for brochure and booking details. **ETC ★★★★★**
e-mail: info@caytontouring.co.uk   **website: www.caytontouring.co.uk**

WETHERBY (near)

Mrs Webb, Maustin Caravan Park, Kearby with Netherby, Near Wetherby LS22 4DA (Tel & Fax: 0113 2886234). Maustin Park offers a peaceful haven for people without family responsibilities. A quiet backwater, situated five miles south of Harrogate in the lower Wharfe Valley, close to Harewood House and many attractions. Tourer field with hook-ups and free showers. Spacious parking around our bowling green. Luxury holiday homes for hire fully equipped to a high standard and including linen. Restored holiday cottage also available. Own a holiday home in prestigious surroundings. Our popular "Stables" restaurant serves excellent food (open Friday to Sunday). Please send for our free brochure. **ETC** ★★★★★ *HOLIDAY PARK,*

DAVID BELLAMY GOLD CONSERVATION AWARD WINNERS.
e-mail: info@maustin.co.uk   website: www.maustin.co.uk

WHITBY

D.I. Jackson, York House Caravan Park, Hawsker, Whitby YO22 4LW (01947 880354). Situated on the North Yorkshire coast in the National Park, with panoramic views over the North Sea, Yorkshire Moors and Whitby. Grass site, mainly level with access roads and clearly defined pitches. Well screened with trees and hedges. Amenities include modern toilet block with showers, sinks, toilets, hot water, washer and spin dryer, and washing up sinks. Electric hook-ups. Shop. Children and pets welcome. Rates from £8 per night. Open March to October inclusive. **AA** *THREE PENNANTS.*

YORK

See also Colour Display Advertisement

York Touring Caravan Site, Greystones Farm, Towthorpe Moor Lane, Near Strensall, York YO32 9ST (01904 499275; Fax: 01904 499271). One mile off A64, signposted Strensall. Secluded spacious Park ideal for exploring historic York and surrounding area. All new facilities including modern shower and toilet chalet with disabled access; laundry room, café, on-site golf range and putting course. Electric hook-ups, water and drainage hook-ups and washing-up area. Pets allowed. Open all year. **ETC** ★★★★, **AA** *FOUR PENNANTS.*
e-mail: info@yorkcaravansite.co.uk
website: www.yorkcaravansite.co.uk

MOOR END FARM
(Established 1965)
Acaster Malbis, York YO23 2UQ. Tel/Fax: 01904 706727

Moor End Farm is a small, family-run caravan and camping site 4 miles south-west of York. The Tourist Board graded site has 10 touring pitches and 6 static caravans. Two of the static caravans are available for holiday lets starting from £40 a night or £200 a week. The hire caravans have colour TV, shower, toilet, fridge, 2 bedrooms, kitchen, dining/living area and accommodate up to 6 persons. Touring facilities available are electric hook-ups, hot showers, toilets, dish-washing sink, fridge/freezer and microwave oven. There are picnic tables around the site for our guests to use. Moor End Farm is on a bus route to York and is 5 minutes' walk from the popular river bus service and the local inn. We are also very close to the York/Selby cycle track and the York park & ride scheme.

See also Colour Display Advertisement

The Alders Caravan Park, Home Farm, Alne, York YO6 11TB (Tel & Fax: 01347 838722). The Alders has been sensitively developed in historic parkland on a working farm where visitors may escape from the hustle and bustle of life to peace and tranquillity. The water meadow, wild flowers and woodland walk combine to offer the nature lover an idyllic environment in which to stay. It is a level, dry site with electric hook-ups, fully equipped shower rooms, telephone and gas; nearby village shop, village cricket, golf and fishing. Near to A1 and A19 but convenient for York, Harrogate, Dales, Moors, Heritage Coast and National Trust properties. Brochure available. ETC ★★★★★

CAMPING SITES

GLAISDALE (Near Whitby)
See also Colour Display Advertisement

Mr and Mrs G Mortimer, Hollins Farm, Glaisdale, Whitby YO21 2PZ (01947 897516). Small farm camp site (TENTS ONLY) in the valley of Glaisdale in the North Yorkshire Moors, nine miles from Whitby. Good walking country. Handy for Whitby, the coastal villages and steam railway. Pony trekking and fishing available. Village amenities include good store and butchers, pubs which serve meals, tennis court. On-site amenities include flush toilet, showers, fridge, shaver point and washing up facilities. Children and pets welcome. Please write with SAE, or telephone for further details. Also good B&B.

HAWES

Mr and Mrs Facer, Bainbridge Ings Caravan and Camping Site, Hawes DL8 3NU (01969 667354). A quiet, clean, family-run site with beautiful views and only half-a-mile from Hawes. Good centre for walking and touring the Dales. Children and pets welcome. You can be assured of a warm welcome. Terms from £9 per day. ETC ★★
e-mail: janet@bainbridge-ings.co.uk **website: www.bainbridge-ings.co.uk**

THE FHG DIPLOMA

HELP IMPROVE BRITISH TOURIST STANDARDS

You are choosing holiday accommodation from our very popular FHG Publications.
Whether it be a hotel, guest house, farmhouse or self-catering accommodation, we think you will find it hospitable, comfortable and clean, and your host and hostess friendly and helpful.

Why not write and tell us about it?

As a recognition of the generally well-run and excellent holiday accommodation reviewed in our publications, we at FHG Publications Ltd. present a diploma to proprietors who receive the highest recommendation from their guests who are also readers of our Guides. If you care to write to us praising the holiday you have booked through FHG Publications Ltd. – whether this be board, self-catering accommodation, a sporting or a caravan holiday, what you say will be evaluated and the proprietors who reach our final list will be contacted.

The winning proprietor will receive an attractive framed diploma to display on his premises as recognition of a high standard of comfort, amenity and hospitality. FHG Publications Ltd. offer this diploma as a contribution towards the improvement of standards in tourist accommodation in Britain. Help your excellent host or hostess to win it!

FHG DIPLOMA

We nominate ....

....

Because

Name ....

Address ....

....

Telephone No...

Aberdeen, Banff & Moray

CARAVANS FOR HIRE

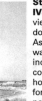

ELGIN

Station Caravan Park, West Beach, Hopeman, Near Elgin IV30 5RU (Tel & Fax: 01343 830880). The park boasts terrific views of the Moray Firth where we often sight the Moray Firth dolphins, and is an ideal place to relax and have a good holiday. As well as the beach, there are caves, rockpools and fossils within walking distance. The village itself has all the shops you will need including a chemist, post office, takeaway food, ice cream, convenience store and pubs. We have luxury caravan holiday homes for hire, many with sea views, plus there are usually a few for sale. For the touring units there are electric hook-ups, water points, modern toilet/shower blocks and a launderette. Open from 28th March till 31st October. For full price information please contact the park direct.

e-mail: stationcaravanpark@talk21.com   **website: www.stationcaravanpark.co.uk**

ENGLAND   Ratings You Can Trust

The English Tourism Council (formerly the English Tourist Board) has joined with the **AA** and **RAC** to create a new, easily understood quality rating for serviced accommodation, giving a clear guide of what to expect.

HOTELS are given a rating from One to Five **Stars**.

GUEST ACCOMMODATION, which includes guest houses, bed and breakfasts, inns and farmhouses, is rated from One to Five **Diamonds**.

HOLIDAY PARKS, TOURING PARKS and CAMPING PARKS – standards of quality range from a One Star (acceptable) to a Five Star (exceptional) park.

SELF-CATERING – the more **Stars** (from One to Five) awarded to an establishment, the higher the levels of quality you can expect. Establishments at higher rating levels also have to meet some additional requirements for facilities.

SCOTLAND

Star Quality Grades will reflect the most important aspects of a visit, such as the warmth of welcome, efficiency and friendliness of service, the quality of the food and the cleanliness and condition of the furnishings, fittings and decor.

THE MORE STARS, THE HIGHER THE STANDARDS.

The description, such as Hotel, Guest House, Bed and Breakfast, Lodge, Holiday Park, Self-catering etc tells you the type of property and style of operation.

WALES

STAR QUALITY GUIDE FOR

HOTELS, GUEST HOUSES AND FARMHOUSES

SELF-CATERING ACCOMMODATION (Cottages, Apartments, Houses)

CARAVAN HOLIDAY HOME PARKS (Holiday Parks, Touring Parks, Camping Parks)

Places which score highly will have an especially welcoming atmosphere and pleasing ambience, high levels of comfort and guest care, and attractive surroundings enhanced by thoughtful design and attention to detail.

Argyll & Bute

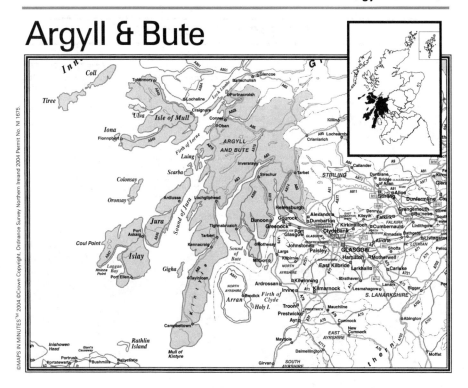

CARAVANS FOR HIRE

TARBERT

Port Ban Caravan Park, Kilberry, Tarbert PA29 6YD (01880 770224; Fax: 01880 770246). Join us at our beautiful seaside park with panoramic views from every caravan. Relax in the peaceful atmosphere, roam along quiet beaches or explore the unspoilt countryside. Alternatively, amuse yourselves with our boating, sports and games facilities or join in our organised activities, with special events for children. Ideally situated for hillwalking and bird spotting. Shop, coffee bar, restaurant and launderette on site. Luxury caravans for sale or hire. Tourers and tents welcome. A friendly welcome awaits you at this family run park.
e-mail: portban@aol.com
website: www.portban.com

HOLIDAY PARKS AND CENTRES

LOCH LOMOND

Loch Lomond Holiday Park, Inveruglas, Argyll & Bute G83 7DW (01301 704224; Fax: 01301 704206). Only a handful of holiday parks in Britain can boast a view which is celebrated in legend and song throughout the world. In the heart of Scotland's first National Park, Loch Lomond Holiday Park is a beautifully landscaped 13 acre park located on the western banks of Loch Lomond at Inveruglas. Just 40 miles from Glasgow and set in stunning surroundings it offers peace and tranquillity from the hustle and bustle of everyday life. STB ★★★★★ HOLIDAY PARK, ★★★★/★★★★★ SELF CATERING
E-mail: enquiries@lochlomond-lodges.co.uk
website: www.lochlomond-caravans.co.uk
www.lochlomond-lodges.co.uk

OBAN

Telephone:
01631 720255/217

Tralee Bay Holidays

Tralee Bay Holidays, Benderloch, by Oban, Argyll PA37 1QR
E-mail: tralee@easynet.co.uk • Website: www.tralee.com

See also Colour Advertisement

CARAVAN SITES AND NIGHT HALTS

Invercoe Highland Holidays, Invercoe, Glencoe PH49 4HP (Tel & Fax: 01855 811210). At Invercoe Highland Holidays we offer you quiet, get-away-from-it-all vacations, in what is one of the most picturesque of the Scottish Glens. You can have a relaxing break in a stone cottage, luxury timber lodge, mobile holiday home or bring your own caravan, tent or tourer for the holiday of your choice. We have been providing holidays for over thirty years and are confident our high standard of accommodation will provide an excellent base to explore the West Highlands. Open all year. **STB ★★★★** *SELF CATERING.*
e-mail: invercoe@sol.co.uk
website: www.invercoe.co.uk

HELENSBURGH (NEAR)

Please mention the
FHG Guide to Caravan & Camping Holidays
when enquiring about accommodation featured in these pages.

🚐 🅢 🛆

OBAN

Howard and Judy Jones, Oban Caravan and Camping Park, Gallanachmore Farm, Oban PA34 (01631 562425; Fax: 01631 566624). In an area of outstanding scenic beauty and graded as "Very Good", Gallanachmore Farm is situated on the seafront overlooking the Island of Kerrera. The Park provides excellent toilet and shower facilities, a well-stocked shop, launderette, children's play area and lends itself superbly for boating, fishing, windsurfing and scuba diving holidays. Also our static park has modern caravans for hire, all with sea views. Situated two-and-a-half miles south of Oban; from roundabout in the centre of the town, follow signs to Gallanach. Terms from £10.00 to £12.50 per night (two persons in touring van, tent or motorhome). **STB ★★★★** *HOLIDAY PARK*
e-mail: info@obancaravanpark.com

CAMPING SITES

🚐 🅢 🛆

KINLOCHLEVEN
See also Colour Display Advertisement

Caolasnacon Caravan & Camping Park, Kinlochleven PA40 4RS. There are 20 static six-berth caravans for holiday hire on this lovely site with breathtaking mountain scenery on the edge of Loch Leven — an ideal touring centre. Caravans have electric lighting, Calor gas cookers and heaters, toilet, shower, fridge and colour TV. There are two toilet blocks with hot water and showers and laundry facilities. Children are welcome and pets allowed. Open from April to October. Milk, gas, soft drinks available on site; shops three miles. Sea loch fishing, hill walking and boating; boats and rods for hire, fishing tackle for sale. Weekly rates for vans from £205; 10% reduction on two-week bookings. Tourers from £9.50 nightly. Seven and a half acres for campers, rates from £6.25 nightly. For details contact **Mrs Patsy Cameron 01855 831279.**

A useful Index of Towns/Villages and Counties appears on page 174 – please also refer to Contents Page 3.

Ayrshire & Arran

HOLIDAY PARKS AND CENTRES

AYR (By)

See also Colour Display Advertisement

Sundrum Castle Holiday Park, Coylton, by Ayr (01292 570057). Award-winning holiday park with great facilities in superb location. In the heart of Burns Country, it is close to Ayr and its popular beaches. Indoor pool, kids' clubs and live entertainment. For a free colour brochure or to make a booking call **Parkdean Holidays** on **0870 420 5607**. STB ★★★★, **AA** *HOLIDAY PARK, THISTLE AWARD*
e-mail: enquiries@parkdeanholidays.co.uk
website: www.parkdeanholidays.co.uk

KILWINNING

See also Colour Display Advertisement

Braemoor Christian Holiday Village, Torranyard, Kilwinning KA13 7RD (01294 850286; Fax: 01294 850486). Set in the heart of the beautiful Ayrshire countryside, offering the highest standard with superbly appointed 6 and 8 berth luxury caravans. Facilities include 25m swimming pool, sauna, steam room, jacuzzi, fitness suite, children's adventure playground, coffee shop and restaurant, bike hire and Hamish Kidz Klub. Sunday services throughout the summer season. STB ★★★★ *HOLIDAY PARK.*
e-mail: info@braemoorchv.com
website: www.braemoorchv.com

Borders

HOLIDAY PARKS AND CENTRES

🚐 💲 ☼

COLDINGHAM

See also Colour Display Advertisement

Scoutscroft Holiday Centre, St Abbs Head, Coldingham TD14 5NB (018907 71338; Reservations: 0800 169 3786). Thistle Awarded Holiday Homes for hire and sale. Toilet and shower facilities with heated family room. Spaciously developed touring plots. Free adult and children's entertainment. Creels Restaurant serving meals throughout the season. Family orientated bars. Scooties Entertainment Bar. Chip shop, burger bar, arcade, play areas and laundry facilities. Sun Lounge, quiet, peaceful and smoke-free extension to Scooties Bar. On-site Dive Centre with unique DIVING PACKAGE.
e-mail: holidays@scoutscroft.co.uk
website: www.scoutscroft.co.uk

CARAVAN SITES AND NIGHT HALTS

💲

DUNS

Mr C. Gregg, Greenlaw Caravan Park, Bank Street, Greenlaw, Duns TD10 6XX (01361 810341). Picturesque riverside park attached to a friendly country village offering shops, hotels and inns with regular functions; ideal for bowling, fishing, golf, walking or simply relaxing. New "Blackadder Touring Park". See otters playing and herons fishing at the waterfall, choice of breathtaking riverside pitches. Well placed for exploring the Borders, the Northumbrian coast, Edinburgh and Newcastle. Short Breaks catered for. Only 37 miles south of Edinburgh on the A697. Winner/Runner up - Most Improved Park in Scotland 2001.
website: www.greenlawcaravanpark.com

Visit the FHG website **www.holidayguides.com**
for details of the wide choice of accommodation
featured in the full range of FHG titles

Dumfries & Galloway

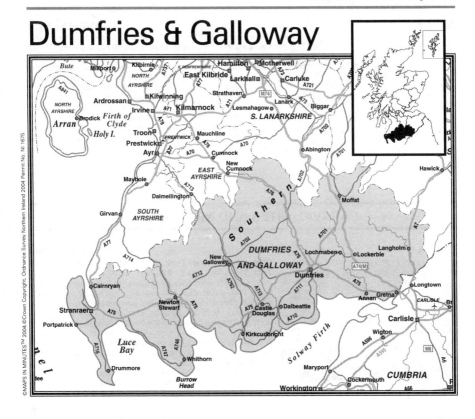

HOLIDAY PARKS AND CENTRES

DUMFRIES (near)

Southerness Holiday Village, near Dumfries (01387 880256). Overlooking two miles of golden sands, with the beautiful Galloway Hills as the backdrop. Indoor heated swimming pool, kids' club and family entertainment. For a free colour brochure or to make a booking call **Parkdean Holidays** on **0870 420 5607. STB ★★★★**
e-mail: **enquiries@parkdeanholidays.co.uk**
website: **www.parkdeanholidays.co.uk**

Shambellie Museum of Costume
Dumfries, Dumfriesshire • 01387 850375
Step back in time and experience Victorian and Edwardian grace and refinement.
Set in attractive wooded grounds,See period clothes in authentic settings.

🚐 🏠 ⛺

PORTPATRICK

Adam and Liz Mackie, Galloway Point Holiday Park, Portpatrick, Stranraer DG9 9AA (01776 810561). This David Bellamy Silver Award park, family-owned and managed, offers panoramic views over the Irish Sea and has a plethora of historic sites and gardens in the area for you to visit. Galloway Point makes an ideal base for touring the area, walking, golf and fishing holidays. We also have new luxurious caravan holiday homes for hire and a small selection for sale. This family-owned park is an excellent choice for short breaks as well as main holidays in Bonnie Galloway. A warm family welcome awaits you. **RAC, AA** *THREE PENNANTS, DAVID BELLAMY SILVER AWARD, BRITISH HOLIDAY & HOME PARKS ASSOCIATION.*

CARAVAN SITES AND NIGHT HALTS

🚐 🏠 ⛺

CREETOWN

Creetown Caravan Park, Silver Street, Creetown DG8 7HU (Tel & Fax: 01671 820377). Situated just off the A75, 6 miles east of Newton Stewart and three miles from the Galloway Forest Park, an ideal base for exploring this scenic area. Village shops and hotels only a two-minute walk. Selection of de luxe six-berth caravans to let, all of an excellent standard and fully-equipped. Heated outdoor swimming pool (seasonal), children's play area, games room with video games and pool tables. Creetown is part of the local designated cycle route. Facilities for touring caravans and tents. Terms available on request. **STB** ★★★★ *HOLIDAY PARK*
e-mail: BeatriceMcneill@btinternet.com
website: www.creetown-caravans.co.uk

☼ 🏠 ⛺

DUMFRIES

See also Colour Display Advertisement

Mr A.J. Wight, Barnsoul Farm, Irongray, Shawhead, Dumfries DG2 9SQ (Tel & Fax: 01387 730453; Tel: 01387 730249). Barnsoul, one of Galloway's most scenic working farms. Bird watching, walking and fishing all available on your doorstep. Fifty pitches available on ten acres. Chalets and Wigwam bunkhouses for rent. Car/caravans £8 to £12, car/tents £8 to £12. Cycle or motorcycle and tent £7 to £10. Open from March to October, at other times by arrangement. *DAVID BELLAMY GOLD AWARD,* **STB** ★★★ *HOLIDAY PARK*
e-mail: barnsouldg@aol.com
website: www.barnsoulfarm.co.uk

🚐 🏠 ⛺

NEWTON STEWART (Glenluce)

Whitecairn Farm Caravan Park, Glenluce, DG8 0NZ (01581 300267). Peacefully set by a quiet country road, one-and-a-half-miles from the village of Glenluce with panoramic views over the rolling Galloway countryside to Luce Bay. This family-run park offers a choice of two different caravan types sleeping up to six, all of a high standard and fully equipped except for linen. Amenities include children's play area, launderette, telephone, toilet blocks and shower rooms. Electric hook-ups on touring pitches. The park offers freedom for children of all ages and dogs are welcome under strict control. Open all year. Colour brochure available. **STB** ★★★★ *HOLIDAY PARK*
e-mail: enquiries@whitecairncaravans.co.uk
website: www.whitecairncaravans.co.uk

Dundee & Angus

CARAVAN SITES AND NIGHT HALTS

BRECHIN

Scott Murray, Eastmill Caravan Park, Brechin DD9 7EL (01356 622810; out of season 01356 622487; Fax: 01356 623356). Beautifully situated on flat grassy site along the River South Esk, within easy access of scenic Angus Glens, local walks and 10 miles from sandy east coast beaches; midway between Dundee and Aberdeen. Shop, gas supplies, shower block, laundry and hook-ups on site; licensed premises nearby. Open April to October. Six-berth caravans with mains services available to rent. Facilities for tourers, caravanettes and tents. Dogs welcome.

Highlands

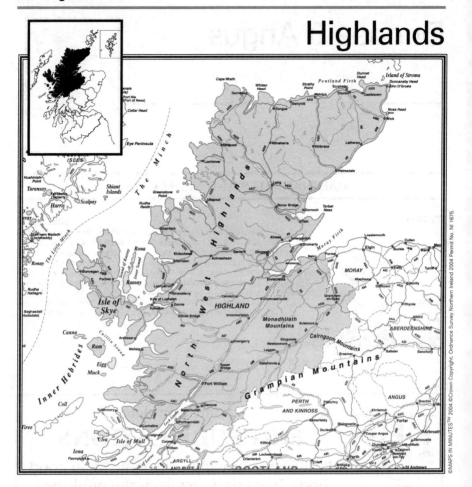

Highlands North

CARAVANS FOR HIRE

NORTH SUTHERLAND (near Bettyhill)

One only residential caravan on quiet site in the Strathnaver Valley, five miles from the coast and Bettyhill village, which has a lovely sandy beach, hotel, cafe, shop, post office, swimming pool, museum and tourist information. Pony trekking and trout fishing are available. The caravan has two bedrooms, one double and one twin. Electric lighting, shower room with wc, kitchen with fridge, gas cooker and heater. It is fully equipped except for bed linen and towels. Open May to September. Terms from £160 to £170 per week. Apply: **Mrs C.M. MacLeod, Achnabourin, Strathnaver, Near Bettyhill, North Sutherland KW11 6UA (01641 561210).**

SCOURIE

Holiday Caravan, Bayview, Badcall, Scourie IV27 4TH. Six-berth caravan with gas cooking, heating, shower and mains electricity. Situated in the beautiful North West Highlands of Scotland, two hours driving time from the city of Inverness. Ideal centre for touring Northern Scotland and the Western Isles (vehicle ferry sails from Ullapool to Stornoway). There are ample opportunities for climbing and hillwalking. Visit the Handa Island bird sanctuary, also local boat trips. Permits available for trout fishing. The scenery around the caravan is breathtaking, and there are many beautiful beaches within a short drive. Contact: **Florence or Bert Macleod (01349 864072).**

HOLIDAY PARKS AND CENTRES

DORNOCH (near)

See also Colour Display Advertisement

Grannie's Heilan' Hame Holiday Park, Near Dornoch (01862 810383). Award-winning holiday park with great facilities in superb location. The park overlooks a beautiful beach and the Dornoch Firth. Indoor pool, kids' club and live entertainment. For a free colour brochure or to make a booking call **Parkdean Holidays** on **0870 420 5607. STB ★★★★, AA** *HOLIDAY PARK, THISTLE AWARD*
e-mail: enquiries@parkdeanholidays.co.uk
website: www.parkdeanholidays.co.uk

CARAVAN SITES AND NIGHT HALTS

JOHN O'GROATS

John O'Groats Caravan and Camping Site, John O'Groats KW1 4YS (Tel & Fax: 01955 611329). At end of A99 on seafront beside "last house in Scotland", caravan and camping site with showers, launderette, electric hook-ups and disabled toilet. Caravans, caravanettes and tents welcome. Booking office for day trips to Orkney Islands on site. Hotel, restaurant, cafe, harbour 150 metres. Magnificent cliff scenery with sea birds galore including puffins, guillemots, skuas within one-and-a-half-miles. Seals are often seen swimming to and fro and there is a seal colony only four miles away. From the site you can see the wide panorama of the Orkney Islands, the nearest of which is only seven miles away. Prices from £8 per night. Public telephone 150 metres. **STB ★★★** *HOLIDAY PARK*
e-mail: info@johnogroatscampsite.co.uk   website: www.johnogroatscampsite.co.uk

Highlands Mid

CARAVAN SITES AND NIGHT HALTS

ACHNASHEEN
See also Colour Display Advertisement

Tony and Ann Davis, Gruinard Bay Caravan Park, Laide IV22 2ND (Tel & Fax: 01445 731225). Situated just a stone's throw from the beach, Gruinard Bay Caravan Park offers the perfect setting for a holiday or a stopover on the West Coast of Scotland. Family-owned and personally operated, the park boasts magnificent views across Gruinard Bay. Sea-front touring pitches, electric hook-ups. No charge for awnings. Camping pitches available. Free toilet and shower facilities, shop - gas available on site. Laundry facilities by request. Static holiday homes available. Pets welcome (not in holiday homes). **STB** ★★★ *HOLIDAY PARK.*
e-mail: gruinard@ecosse.net
website: www.highlandbreaks.net

SHIELBRIDGE (Glen Shiel)
Shiel Caravan Site, Shielbridge, By Kyle (01599 511221). Touring site situated at the west end of the spectacular Glen Shiel on the A87 Fort William to Kyle of Lochalsh road (access by shop at Shielbridge). This is an ideal centre from which to explore the beautiful West Coast and is 15 miles from the Isle of Skye bridge at Kyle. There is space for 25 caravans and 50 tents; all usual facilities including showers. Shop and snack bar adjacent, gas and petrol available. The site is open from March 16th to October 16th. Toilet and shower block incorporating drying facilities. Children and pets welcome. New shower block and electricity for caravans planned for Spring 2004. Rates from £4 per person per night.

Highlands South

CARAVANS FOR HIRE

INVERGARRY
Mrs P. Fraser, Allt-Na-Sithean, South Laggan, By Spean Bridge PH34 4EA (01809 501311). Enjoy a holiday in the most beautiful part of the Highlands. There is a wonderful view down the valley towards Loch Lochy. The Caledonian Canal is within walking distance, you can go hill climbing, walking, fishing or golfing. Visit Skye, Aviemore, Inverness and the West Highlands. Fort William 20 miles, Invergarry village three miles. The caravan is equipped for four people. Shower and toilet, gas cooker, gas fire, fridge, microwave, colour TV. Duvets or blankets supplied. Bed linen supplied for two people. Sorry - no pets. Non-smokers preferred. Open May till October. Rates from £120 to £180 per week. Please telephone for further details.

HOLIDAY PARKS AND CENTRES

SPEYSIDE LEISURE PARK

Self-Catering Holidays in the Heart of the Highlands

The park is situated in a quiet riverside setting with mountain views, only a short walk from Aviemore centre and shops. We offer a range of warm, well equipped chalets, cabins and caravans, including a caravan for the disabled. Prices include electricity, gas, linen, towels and use of our heated indoor pool, sauna and gym. There are swings, a climbing frame and low level balance beams for the children. Permit fishing is available on the river. Discounts are given on some local attractions.

Families, couples or groups will find this an ideal location for a wide range of activities including:

* *Horse riding* • *Golfing* • *Fishing* • *Hillwalking* • *RSPB Reserves*
* *Mountain and Watersports* • *Reindeer herd* • *Steam railway and the Whisky Trail*

Only slightly further afield there are many places of interest such as Culloden Moor, Fort George and of course, the not to be missed, Loch Ness. Accommodation sleeps from 4-8, but we offer a reduced rate for a couple. Short Breaks are available. Sorry, no pets, except guide and hearing dogs.

Speyside Leisure Park
Dalfaber Road, Aviemore,
Inverness-shire PH22 1PX

Tel: 01479 810236
Fax: 01479 811688

E-mail: fhg@speysideleisure.com
www.speysideleisure.com

See also Colour Advertisement

e-mail: info@auchnahillin.co.uk

INVERNESS (Near)

Auchnahillin Caravan & Camping Park, Daviot East, Inverness IV2 5XQ (01463 772286; Fax: 01463 772282). Friendly, informal family-run ten-acre park, set in tranquil glen with fine views, yet conveniently located just off the A9, only seven miles south of Inverness with several other popular destinations being within an easy drive. Informative reception area, small shop, children's play area, laundry and dishwashing facilities, showers, toilets and hairdryers. Disabled facilities. Bar and restaurant. 12 fully equipped, self-contained static caravan/chalet holiday homes for hire, £29 to £58 per night/£145 to £290 per week. 45 pitches for touring units, £8 to £10 per night. Camping ground for up to 30 tents, £4 to £9 per night. Dogs welcome. Open 15th March until 31st October. Chalet also available for winter lets.
STB ★★★★ *HOLIDAY PARK*
website: www.auchnahillin.co.uk

The Loch Ness Monster Visitor Centre
Drumnadrochit, Inverness • 01456 450342
website: www.lochness-centre.com
All you ever wanted to know about the monster! Superb documentary,
including eye-witness accounts. Shop with souvenirs.

See also Colour Display Advertisement

Nairn Lochloy Holiday Park (01667 453764). Nestling between the sand dunes of East Nairn Beach, a beautiful marina and a championship golf course. Indoor heated pool, kids' club and family entertainment. For a free colour brochure or to make a booking call **Parkdean Holidays** on **0870 420 5607. STB** ★★★★

e-mail: **enquiries@parkdeanholidays.co.uk**
website: **www.parkdeanholidays.co.uk**

CARAVAN SITES AND NIGHT HALTS

ARISAIG

A. Simpson, Camusdarach, Arisaig, Inverness-shire PH39 4NT (01687 450221). 'Camusdarach' is the ideal base to explore the beautiful scenery of the 'Road to the Isles' and the West Highlands. The grassy site, surrounded by mature trees, has 42 pitches for tents or vans including 16 electric hook-ups. A unique shower/toilet block has sheltered washing-up sinks, a laundry and a separate room with disabled and baby changing facilities. A foot path leads you on the short walk to the fabulous beaches featured in 'Local Hero'. Local shops, restaurants and ferries are within easy reach at Arisaig (four miles) and Mallaig (six miles). Traigh Golf Course is only one mile away. Pitch fees, based on two people with car: tents from £10 per night, caravans from £12 per night, serviced pitches available. *ASSC MEMBER*
e-mail: **camdarach@aol.com**
website: **www.camusdarach.com**

BEAULY

Cannich Caravan & Camping Park, Cannich, by Beauly IV4 7NL (01456 415364). Cannich Caravan Park lies at the head of Glen Affric and is an ideal base to explore this most beautiful of glens with its majestic Scots pines, sparkling lochs and rugged mountains. Suitable for caravans, motorhomes and tents, choose from open grassy pitches or the shelter of the Scots pines that abound in the park. Comfortable, luxury, fully equipped static caravans are available for weekly or nightly hire. Free showers, indoor washing up, laundry, TV room, playpark, ON-SITE BIKE HIRE. **STB** ★★★★, **AA** *THREE PENNANTS*
e-mail: **enquiries@highlandcamping.co.uk**
website: **www.highlandcamping.co.uk**

FHG

FHG PUBLICATIONS

publish a large range of well-known accommodation guides. We will be happy to send you details or you can use the order form at the back of this book.

Perth & Kinross

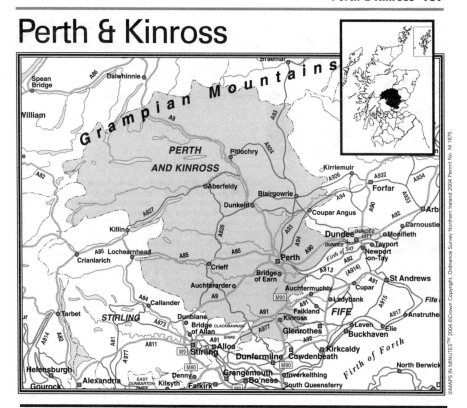

HOLIDAY PARKS AND CENTRES

☀ 🚐 💲 🏕

PITLOCHRY (near)

See also Colour Display Advertisement

Tummel Valley Holiday Park, Tummel Bridge, Near Pitlochry (01882 634221). Award-winning holiday park with great facilities in superb location on the banks of the River Tummel. Indoor pool and live entertainment. For more details of this park and offers throughout the UK, to order a free colour brochure, or to make a booking call: **Parkdean Holidays** on **0870 420 5607. STB ★★★★, AA** HOLIDAY PARK, THISTLE AWARD

e-mail: **enquiries@parkdeanholidays.co.uk**
website: **www.parkdeanholidays.co.uk**

CARAVAN SITES AND NIGHT HALTS

🚐 💲 🏕

COMRIE (near Crieff)

P.J., E.L & P.P. Gill, West Lodge Caravan Park, Comrie PH6 2LS (01764 670354). Pleasant family-run caravan and camping park. Good touring area. Excellent facilities on the park including flush toilets, free hot showers, laundry area, shop, gas and telephone. Pitches have electric hook-ups. Six six-berth static vans for hire, all with toilet and running water, and showers. Children and pets welcome. Caravan hire from £180 to £260 per week; £28 to £40 per night. Touring vans and motor homes £10 per night including electricity, tents £8 to £10. Prior booking required July and August. Open 1st April to 31st October. Ring for information, brochure sent on request. **STB ★★★★** HOLIDAY PARK

KINLOCH RANNOCH
Kilvrecht Caravan Park, Loch Rannoch, Perthshire PH8 0JR (01350 727284; Fax: 01350 727811). Secluded campsite on a level open area in quiet and secluded woodland setting. There is fishing available for brown trout on Loch Rannoch. Several trails begin from the campsite. Please write, fax or telephone for further information.
e-mail: hamish.murray@forestry.gsi.gov.uk

PITLOCHRY
Milton of Fonab Caravan Park, Pitlochry PH16 5NA (01796 472882; Fax: 01796 474363). A 16 acre site with 154 touring pitches (last arrival 9pm) with electricity and awnings extra and 36 caravans to let, sleep six (minimum let two nights) with mains water, shower, toilet, TV, etc. Site facilities include showers, electric hook-ups, chemical disposal point, telephone, shop, etc. Shops and eating out places one mile. We also take tents. Fishing available. Children and pets welcome. Caravans from £250 to £380 per week; pitches from £11 per night. Open March to October. **STB ★★★★** *HOLIDAY PARK*
e-mail: info@fonab.co.uk
website: www.fonab.co.uk

Stirling &
The Trossachs

CARAVAN SITES AND NIGHT HALTS

DOLLAR
Mrs A. Small, Riverside Caravan Park, Dollar FK14 7LX (01259 742896). Site of seven acres - 30 statics (not for hire), 30 touring vans/tents. Grassy, level pitches on riverbank. Situation on B913, half-a-mile south of Dollar, which is an attractive hillfoot town with steeply wooded glen dominated by Castle Campbell. Ideal for anglers and hillwalkers and a central base from which to tour the area. Site facilities include toilets, showers, Calor gas sales, electric hook-up points. Free fishing on site; golf, swimming, riding available nearby. Pets welcome. Open April to September. Brochure and tariff available on request.

Scottish Islands

Orkney

CARAVAN SITES AND NIGHT HALTS

PUBLISHER'S NOTE

While every effort is made to ensure accuracy, we regret that FHG Publications cannot accept responsibility for errors, misrepresentations or omissions in our entries or any consequences thereof. Prices in particular should be checked because we go to press early. We will follow up complaints but cannot act as arbiters or agents for either party.

Visit the FHG website **www.holidayguides.com**
for details of the wide choice of accommodation
featured in the full range of FHG titles

Ratings You Can Trust

ENGLAND

The English Tourism Council (formerly the English Tourist Board) has joined with the **AA** and **RAC** to create a new, easily understood quality rating for serviced accommodation, giving a clear guide of what to expect.

HOTELS are given a rating from One to Five **Stars** – the more Stars, the higher the quality and the greater the range of facilities and level of services provided.

GUEST ACCOMMODATION, which includes guest houses, bed and breakfasts, inns and farmhouses, is rated from One to Five **Diamonds**. Progressively higher levels of quality and customer care must be provided for each one of the One to Five Diamond ratings.

HOLIDAY PARKS, TOURING PARKS and CAMPING PARKS are now also assessed using **Stars**. Standards of quality range from a One Star (acceptable) to a Five Star (exceptional) park.

Look out also for the new **SELF-CATERING** Star ratings. The more **Stars** (from One to Five) awarded to an establishment, the higher the levels of quality you can expect. Establishments at higher rating levels also have to meet some additional requirements for facilities.

SCOTLAND

Star Quality Grades will reflect the most important aspects of a visit, such as the warmth of welcome, efficiency and friendliness of service, the quality of the food and the cleanliness and condition of the furnishings, fittings and decor.

THE MORE STARS,
THE HIGHER THE STANDARDS.

The description, such as Hotel, Guest House, Bed and Breakfast, Lodge, Holiday Park, Self-catering etc tells you the type of property and style of operation.

WALES

Places which score highly will have an especially welcoming atmosphere and pleasing ambience, high levels of comfort and guest care, and attractive surroundings enhanced by thoughtful design and attention to detail

STAR QUALITY GUIDE FOR

HOTELS, GUEST HOUSES AND FARMHOUSES

SELF-CATERING ACCOMMODATION
(Cottages, Apartments, Houses)

CARAVAN HOLIDAY HOME PARKS
(Holiday Parks, Touring Parks, Camping Parks)

★★★★★   *Exceptional quality*
★★★★   *Excellent quality*
★★★   *Very good quality*
★★   *Good quality*
★   *Fair to good quality*

In England, Scotland and Wales, all graded properties are inspected annually by Tourist Authority trained Assessors.

Anglesey & Gwynedd

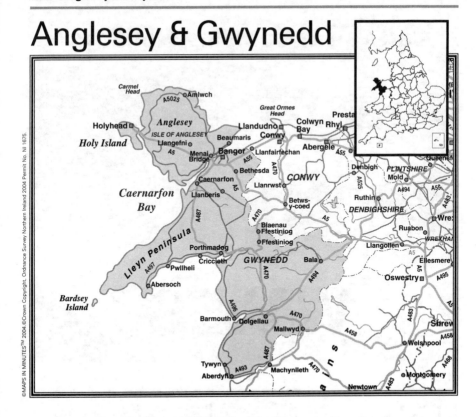

CARAVANS FOR HIRE

PWLLHELI

Mrs Susan Harrison, Cerniog Isaf, Mynydd Nefyn, Pwllheli LL53 6TL (01766 810606). Six-berth caravan set in its own grassed area surrounded by stunning views, with two bedrooms, lounge, kitchen, shower room and toilet. Situated on a small farm, surrounded on all sides by our own land and approached by a private, well maintained drive from the road. As we are two fields away from the road it makes a safe place for children to be free and happy, and as there is no passing traffic it is very peaceful, a wonderful place to unwind and relax. Pwllheli seven miles, Caernarfon 20, Porthmadog 20 and Morfa Nefyn four miles.

HOLIDAY PARKS AND CENTRES

CARAVAN SITES AND NIGHT HALTS

ANGLESEY

Mr & Mrs J.E. & E.W. Hunt, Tyddyn Isaf Caravan Park, Lligwy Bay, Dulas, Anglesey LL70 9PQ (01248 410203; Fax: 01248 410667). Tyddyn Isaf is an award-winning superior park which has been described as a 'wild life wonderland' by David Bellamy. Touring caravans and tents are catered for by the high standard of facilities - "Loo of the Year" award. The site facilities include sanitation, water, electricity, gas, shop, swings, licensed club, take-away food and laundry facilities. The safe, sandy beach can be reached directly from the site (150 yards) and there are swimming baths aplenty on Anglesey. Golf, tennis, fishing, riding and bathing all within easy reach. Half-an-hour's drive to Snowdonia National Park. Open from 1st March to 31st October. Children welcome. Pets by arrangement. Tourers from £12. Six acres for campers from £8 per tent. **WTB ★★★★★,**
DAVID BELLAMY GOLD AWARD, **AA** *FOUR PENNANTS, CALOR GAS 'FINALIST' BEST TOURING PARK IN WALES*
website: www.tyddynisaf.demon.co.uk

BARMOUTH
See also Colour Display Advertisement

Hendre Mynach Touring Caravan and Camping Park, Barmouth LL42 1YR (01341 280262). Situated in southern Snowdonia, close to the beautiful Mawddach Estuary. 100 yards from safe sandy beach. Excellent base for walking and cycling, close to Cycle Route 8. All modern amenities. Hard standings available. Pets welcome, dog walk on site. Approximately 20 minutes pleasant walk along promenade to Barmouth town centre. Bus service and train station close by. Open 1st March - 9th January. Special offers available Spring and Autumn. Phone for colour brochure. Voted AA Best Campsite in Wales 2001.
e-mail: mynach@lineone.net
website: www.hendremynach.co.uk

MERIONETH

See also Colour Display Advertisement

Islawrffordd Caravan Park, Tal-y-Bont, Merioneth LL43 2BQ (01341 247269; Fax: 01341 242639). Situated on the Snowdonia coastline just north of Barmouth, our park offers a limited number of caravans for hire, most of which come with double glazing and central heating along with laundered bedding. Our touring caravan field has been modernised to super pitch quality including hard standing with each plot being reservable. Camping is also available on a first come first served basis. Park facilities include shop, laundry, indoor heated pool, bar, amusements and food bars. Enquiries regarding any of the above to **John or Jane.**
e-mail: info@islawrffordd.co.uk
website: www.islawrffordd.co.uk

PORTHMADOG

Mrs Catherine Wright, Tyddyn Llwyn Caravan Park and Hotel, Black Rock Road, Porthmadog LL49 9UR (01766 512205; Fax: 01766 514601). Situated within 10 minutes' walk of town and close to beach, golf club and water sports. A family park with electric hook-up, shop and gas bottle exchange. Limited number of super pitches. Free hot water and showers are available with facilities for dishwashing, a laundry, TV room with a pool table. Licensed bar and restaurant. There is also a play area for children. Barbecues are allowed and pets are welcome. Tent pitches from £9, touring pitches from £11. Brochure and full tariff on request.
e-mail: info@tyddynllwyn.com
website: www.tyddynllwyn.com

🚐 🅢 🛆   **SNOWDONIA**

Bryn Gloch Caravan and Camping Park, Betws Garmon, Near Caernarfon LL54 7YY (01286 650216; Fax: 01286 650591). Award-winning family-run park within Snowdonia National Park. Nestled between Snowdonia mountain ranges and on the banks of the River Gwyrfai with breathtaking views. Clean, peaceful site, electric hook-ups, luxury toilet/showers and launderette, mother and baby changing room, shop and off-licence, games room, spacious play area, fishing and mini-golf. Footpath to Snowdon two-and-a-half miles, a pub and restaurant within one mile. Many local attractions close by, plus watersports, climbing, walking, horseriding and much more. Modern Caravans, Touring Pitches, Tent Pitches and Self-catering Accommodation. Open all year. **WTB ★★★★, AA** *FOUR PENNANTS*.

e-mail: eurig@bryngloch.co.uk   **website: www.bryngloch.co.uk**

CAMPING SITES

🅢 🛆   **DOLGELLAU**

Mrs Helen Rowlands, Llwyn-Yr-Helm Farm, Brithdir, Dolgellau LL40 2SA (01341 450254). Situated on a minor road half a mile off B4416 which is a loop road between A470 and A494, this is a quiet, small working farm site, four miles from Dolgellau in beautiful countryside, ideal for walking and mountain biking. Many places of interest in the area including slate mines, narrow gauge railways, lakes and mountains and nine miles from sandy beaches. Toilet block with free showers and hot water; shaving points and plug. Facilities for the disabled. Caravans, Dormobiles and tents; electric hook-ups. Pets welcome. Open Easter to November.

🚐 🛆   **TAL-Y-LLYN (Tywyn)**

M. Rees, Dôl-Einion, Tal-y-Llyn, Tywyn LL36 9AJ (01654 761312). Dôl-Einion is perhaps the prettiest campsite in the Snowdonia National Park. It is a flat three acre meadow bordered by colourful rhododendrons in season and there is an attractive trout stream. The site nestles at the foot of mighty Cader Idris, at the start of the main path to the summit. Easy access on B4405 for caravans, camping vans. Hard standing area useful in bad weather. Hook - ups available. Good centre for walking or touring. Castle, narrow gauge railway and lake fishing nearby. On a bus route. Pub and restaurant at walking distance. Toilets and showers. Managed by resident owner. Terms on application.

🅢 🛆   **TREARDDUR BAY**

See also Colour Display Advertisement

Tyn Rhôs Camping Site, Ravenspoint Road, Trearddur Bay, Holyhead, Isle of Anglesey LL65 2AX (01407 860369). A long established camping and touring site. Hot showers, toilets, chemical disposal, electric hook-ups etc. Separate rally field available. Rural location within walking distance of beautiful seaside resort. Perfect for out of season tranquillity, weekend breaks or family holidays. With bathing, sailing, fishing, diving, horse riding, golf, birdwatching, climbing, walking etc nearby, there's something for everyone, even a day trip to Ireland! A55 across Anglesey, Junction 3 to Valley, left at traffic lights onto B4545 for Trearddur Bay. Turn left onto Ravenspoint Road. One mile to shared entrance, take left branch. **WTB ★★**

North Wales

CARAVANS FOR HIRE

Mr and Mrs T.P. Williams, Pen Isaf Caravan Park, Llangernyw, Abergele LL22 8RN (01745 860276).
This small caravan site is situated in beautiful unspoilt countryside, 10 miles from the coast and 12 miles from Betws-y-coed, ideal for touring North Wales. The six-berth caravans are fully equipped except for linen and towels and have shower, flush toilets, hot and cold water, Calor gas cooker, electric light and fridge. Children especially will enjoy a holiday here, there being ample play space and facilities for fishing and pony riding. Pets are allowed but must be kept under control. Open from March to October. Terms on application. SAE please.

HOLIDAY PARKS AND CENTRES

One child FREE with two paying adults. Guide dogs welcome at
Alice in Wonderland Centre
see our **READERS' OFFER VOUCHERS** for details

---

visit the FHG website www.holidayguides.com

Ceredigion

CARAVANS FOR HIRE

ABERPORTH

Mrs S. Jones, Manorafon Caravan Park, Sarnau, Llandyssul SA44 6QH (01239 810564). Sleeps 6. Quiet, peaceful site of five caravans and two log chalets, fully equipped including linen (except towels); all caravans six-berth with end bedrooms. All essential facilities provided. Bathroom facilities with hot water on tap in each van; Calor gas cooker, electric lighting and heating. Toilets and washbasins, showers, shaving points. Calor and Camping Gaz sold. Available March to January. Children welcome. Only half-a-mile from the pleasant Penbryn beach and nine miles from the market towns of Cardigan and Newcastle Emlyn. Half-acre for campers and tourers.
e-mail: info@manorafonholidaypark.co.uk
website: www.manorafonholidaypark.co.uk

CARAVAN SITES AND NIGHT HALTS

LLANGRANNOG

Mr T. Hill, Maes Glas Caravan Park, Penbryn, Sarnau, Llandysul, Dyfed SA44 6QE (Tel & Fax: 01239 654268) This family-owned park is situated in the unspoilt valley leading down to Penbryn Beach. The Park is sheltered yet has views out to sea. We have a modern holiday home for hire as well as a 4-star holiday cottage. Tents and tourers welcome. Located in an Area of Outstanding Natural Beauty, Maes Glas is an ideal location for family holidays and also walking holidays; short breaks available early and late season. A warm welcome awaits you. *DAVID BELLAMY GOLD CONSERVATION AWARD. BRITISH HOLIDAY & HOME PARKS ASSOCIATION.*
e-mail: enquiries@maesglascaravanpark.co.uk
website: www.maesglascaravanpark.co.uk

Pembrokeshire

CARAVANS FOR HIRE

HAVERFORDWEST

CARAVAN SITES AND NIGHT HALTS

FRESHWATER EAST

Mrs M. A. Phillips, Upper Portclew Farm, Freshwater East, Pembroke SA71 5LA (01646 672112). Situated within walking distance across sand dunes to the beach and pub, this site has lovely sea views. Facilities include three showers, three washbasins and six toilets; laundry; electric hook-ups. Dogs welcome. Mini Market. Lamphey one-and-a-half miles. Pembroke three miles, Tenby 10 miles. Many beaches and activities in the area. Touring caravans £12, caravanettes £10, camping site £8, including electric hook-up.

HAVERFORDWEST

Messrs Rowe, Brandy Brook Caravan and Camping Site, Rhyndaston, Hayscastle, Haverfordwest SA62 5PT (01348 840272). This is a small, secluded site in very attractive surroundings, a quiet valley with a trout stream. The ideal situation for the true country lover. Campers are welcome; tents from £4.00 per night including car. Hot water/showers on site. Car essential to get the most from your holiday. Children welcome, pets accepted. Take A487 from Haverfordwest, turn right at Roch Motel, signposted from turning.
e-mail: f.m.rowe@btopenworld.com

🚐 ☼ 🅢 ⛺

LITTLE HAVEN

Mr and Mrs D. James, Hasguard Cross Caravan Park, Little Haven, Haverfordwest SA62 3SL (Tel & Fax: 01437 781443). The Park is situated in the centre of Pembrokeshire National Park, on the Dale peninsula, within easy reach of the many beaches, coastal walks and water sports. The Park covers three-and-a-quarter acres of level grassland tastefully screened with trees, with beautiful views of the countryside overlooking Milford Haven and St Brides Bay. The Park caters for the hire of modern holiday homes with colour TV; touring and motor caravans have electric hook-ups available and the usual facilities. A warm welcome in the Hasguard Inn awaits you where good food and beer is available every evening.

Powys

CARAVANS FOR HIRE

e-mail: info@pinescaravanpark.co.uk

RHAYADER

Ron and Ann Goulding, The Pines Caravan Park, Doldowlod, Llandrindod Wells LD1 6NN (01597 810068). Small, peaceful, family-run park, with views in glorious mid-Wales. Situated on A470 four miles south of Rhayader – a good central position for exploring the Elan and Wye Valleys, the Elan Valley Dams and Reservoirs being approximately five miles away. Nearby there are opportunities for fishing, horse riding, golf etc. A bird watchers' paradise, with many varieties of birds including the Red Kite. Adjacent: inn restaurant and shop. Luxury modern holiday homes for hire and for sale. Fully equipped with shower, flush toilet, hot and cold water, cooker, fridge, colour TV and duvets with covers. Weekly hire terms from £190 per week. Mid-week bookings accepted. Please send for brochure. *DAVID BELLAMY GOLD CONSERVATION AWARD PARK.*
website: www.pinescaravanpark.co.uk

Powis Castle and Garden
Near Welshpool, Powys • 01938 554336
Perched on a rock above gardens of great historical and horticultural importance, the medieval castle contains a superb collection of paintings and furniture and a collection of treasures from India.

King Arthur's Labyrinth
Machynlleth, Powys • 01654 761584
website: www.kingarthurslabyrinth.com
A boat ride along a beautiful subterranean river takes you to the Labyrinth, carved from rock, where the tales of King Arthur are re-told. New 'Bard's Quest' challenges you to go in search of the lost legends hidden in the Maze of Time.

South Wales

HOLIDAY PARKS AND CENTRES

Trecco Bay Holiday Park, near Porthcawl (01656 782103).
A perfect fun-filled family holiday destination with sandy beaches.
Indoor tropical pool complex, kids' clubs and family
entertainment. For a free colour brochure or to make a booking
call **Parkdean Holidays** on **0870 420 5607**. WTB ★★★
e-mail: enquiries@parkdeanholidays.co.uk
website: www.parkdeanholidays.co.uk

CARAVAN SITES AND NIGHT HALTS

GOWER
**Hillend Caravan Park, Llangenith, Gower SA3 1JD (Tel &
Fax: 01792 386204).** Hillend is located on the western tip of the
Gower Peninsula, Britain's first designated Area of Outstanding
Natural Beauty. The 14-acre level campsite nestles at the foot of
Rhossili Down and is one kilometre from the village of
Llangennith. One of the UK's premier surfing beaches, the
magnificent Rhossili Bay is 100 metres from the campsite, making
this an ideal location for water sports enthusiasts and also for
walkers who wish to discover for themselves Gower's
breathtaking and varied coastline. SAE, please for brochure.

MERTHYR TYDFIL

Grawen Caravan and Camping Park, Grawen Farm, Cwm-Taff, Cefn Coed, Merthyr Tydfil CF48 2HS (01685 723740). Clean modern facilities. Picturesque surroundings with forest, mountain, reservoir walks from site. Reservoir trout fishing. Ideally located for touring, visiting places of historic interest and enjoying scenic views. Available April to October. Easy access A470 Brecon Beacons road, one-and-a-half miles Cefn Coed, three-and-a-half miles Merthyr Tydfil, two miles from A456 known as the Heads of the Valleys. Pets welcome. Terms from £8 per night for tent for two persons plus 50p per child. Caravans from £9 per night for two persons plus 50p per child (includes caravan and car).16 electric hook-ups. **WTB ★★★**
e-mail: **grawen.touring@virgin.net**
website: **www.walescaravanandcamping.com**

SWANSEA

See also Colour Display Advertisement

Pitton Cross Caravan & Camping Park, Rhossili, Swansea SA3 1PH (01792 390 593: Fax: 01792 391 010). Pitton Cross Caravan & Camping Park occupies a flat site close to the village of Rhossili. Comprising six small fields each with 15-20 pitches, some with sea views, others offering peace and privacy. Convenient water and hook-up points. 'Dog free' and 'families only' areas. Clean modern shower and utility block, dish washing area, laundry room, parent and toddler room with baby bath and changing facilities. On-site shop for food and other essentials. Breathtaking coastal scenery, unrivalled countryside and fabulous sunsets. Walking, water sports, rock climbing, cycling. See our kite centre for an extensive range of kites. Also fishing tackle and a selection of gifts and crafts.
website: **www.pittoncross.co.uk**

Northern Ireland

County Antrim

CARAVAN SITES AND NIGHT HALTS

£ Å **ANTRIM**

Sixmilewater Caravan Park. The Sixmilewater Caravan Park is pleasantly landscaped, situated close to the shores of Lough Neagh in historic Antrim - an area steeped in history and natural beauty with many attractions and activities for the holidaymaker to enjoy. Facilities include modern toilet and shower block, a fully equipped laundry and electric hook-up for eighteen pitches. The site is ideal for accommodating touring caravans, motor vans and tents and is open from Easter to mid-September. Bookings and reservations can be made at the **Antrim Forum Leisure Centre (028 9446 4131)** or for further information contact: **Antrim Information Centre, 16 High Street, Antrim (028 9442 8331).**
e-mail: info@antrim.gov.uk

£ Å **BALLYMONEY**

Drumaheglis Marina and Caravan Park, 36 Glenstall Road, Ballymoney BT53 7QN (028 276 66466/60227) Situated four miles from Ballymoney just off the A26, this is one of the few, and most attractive access points to the River Bann, with the superb natural environment making it the perfect riverside location. The complex incorporates a boat park, slipway, jetty and overnight berthing facilities. The on-site waterski school is a haven for all disciplines of water-based activities and is the only ski school in Northern Ireland to cater for the disabled. With the Causeway Coast and Antrim Glens close at hand, Drumaheglis is the ideal holiday base. Facilities include: volleyball, table tennis, toilets, showers, laundry, picnic plus barbecue areas, children's play area, woodland walk. Open March to October. Pets welcome (must be kept on lead). **NITB ★★★★★**

e-mail: helen.neill@ballymoney.gov.uk   **website: www.ballymoney.gov.uk**

County Down

CARAVAN SITES AND NIGHT HALTS

£ Å **ROSTREVOR**

Kilbroney Caravan Park, Shore Road, Rostrevor BT34 3ET (028 417 38134). Located approximately half-a-mile from Rostrevor on the main A2 route to Kilkeel, there are few parklands which could surpass the beauty of Kilbroney Park. Nestled between the magnificent Mourne Mountains and Carlingford Lough, Kilbroney has vast areas of open space, riverside walks, play areas, tennis courts, an information area with viewing balcony, a barbecue and a cafe/restaurant. Kilbroney Park offers the camper and caravanner excellent facilities, including serviced on-site hook-ups, laundry facilities and toilet/amenity block. For further details and reservation please contact the park warden.
e-mail: info@newryandmourne.gov.uk
website: www.seenewryandmourne.com

County Tyrone

CARAVAN SITES AND NIGHT HALTS

DUNGANNON

Dungannon Park Caravan and Camping, Dungannon. Set in 70 acres of beautiful parkland surrounding an idyllic stillwater lake, the caravan park is situated in the heartland of Ulster, less than one mile away from the motorway to Belfast, and is within easy walking distance of the town of Dungannon. Relax and enjoy the many facilities available - miles of scenic park walks, barbecue site and picnic area and children's play area. We have twelve fully serviced caravan sites and ample space for tents. Gamewater fly fishery. Terms: Caravans £12 per night, Tents £8. ✓✓✓✓, **AA** *THREE PENNANTS*. For more information contact: **Dungannon and South Tyrone Borough Council (028 8772 7327; Fax: 028 8772 9169).**
e-mail: dungannonpark@utvinternet.com

Republic of Ireland

County Mayo

CARAVAN SITES AND NIGHT HALTS

BALLINA

Mrs Lenahan, Belleek Caravan and Camping Park, Ballina, County Mayo. (00353 96 71533). Belleek Park is located in a quiet woodside setting just two miles from Ballina town and the magnificent River Moy which is Ireland's most prolific salmon river. Facilities for tourers and campers include luxury toilet/shower block, TV and games rooms, laundry, campers' kitchen, tennis court, barbecue area, shop. OUR LUXURY MOBILE HOMES AND APARTMENTS ARE FULLY SERVICED WITH SHOWER, TOILET, KITCHEN AND TELEVISION. A high standard of cleanliness is maintained throughout the park. Belleek Caravan Park provides an ideal location from which to tour the North West of Ireland and guarantees a warm welcome and excellent service. Colour brochure on request. ITB ★★★★
e-mail: lenahan@indigo.ie
website: http://indigo.ie/~lenahan/

Index of towns and counties
Please also refer to Contents on page 3.

THE FHG DIPLOMA

HELP IMPROVE
BRITISH TOURIST STANDARDS

You are choosing holiday accommodation from our very popular FHG Publications.
Whether it be a hotel, guest house, farmhouse or self-catering accommodation, we think you
will find it hospitable, comfortable and clean, and your host and hostess friendly and helpful.

Why not write and tell us about it?

As a recognition of the generally well-run and excellent holiday accommodation reviewed in our
publications, we at FHG Publications Ltd. present a diploma to proprietors who receive the
highest recommendation from their guests who are also readers of our Guides. If you care to
write to us praising the holiday you have booked through FHG Publications Ltd. – whether this
be board, self-catering accommodation, a sporting or a caravan holiday, what you say will be
evaluated and the proprietors who reach our final list will be contacted.

The winning proprietor will receive an attractive framed diploma to display on his premises as
recognition of a high standard of comfort, amenity and hospitality. FHG Publications Ltd. offer
this diploma as a contribution towards the improvement of standards in tourist accommodation
in Britain. Help your excellent host or hostess to win it!

FHG DIPLOMA

We nominate ....

....

Because ....

....

....

Name ....

Address ....

....

Telephone No...

Ratings You Can Trust

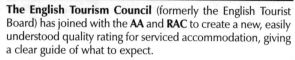

The English Tourism Council (formerly the English Tourist Board) has joined with the **AA** and **RAC** to create a new, easily understood quality rating for serviced accommodation, giving a clear guide of what to expect.

HOTELS are given a rating from One to Five **Stars** – the more Stars, the higher the quality and the greater the range of facilities and level of services provided.

GUEST ACCOMMODATION, which includes guest houses, bed and breakfasts, inns and farmhouses, is rated from One to Five **Diamonds**. Progressively higher levels of quality and customer care must be provided for each one of the One to Five Diamond ratings.

HOLIDAY PARKS, TOURING PARKS and CAMPING PARKS are now also assessed using **Stars**. Standards of quality range from a One Star (acceptable) to a Five Star (exceptional) park.

Look out also for the new **SELF-CATERING** Star ratings. The more **Stars** (from One to Five) awarded to an establishment, the higher the levels of quality you can expect. Establishments at higher rating levels also have to meet some additional requirements for facilities.

SCOTLAND

Star Quality Grades will reflect the most important aspects of a visit, such as the warmth of welcome, efficiency and friendliness of service, the quality of the food and the cleanliness and condition of the furnishings, fittings and decor.

THE MORE STARS,
THE HIGHER THE STANDARDS.

The description, such as Hotel, Guest House, Bed and Breakfast, Lodge, Holiday Park, Self-catering etc tells you the type of property and style of operation.

WALES

Places which score highly will have an especially welcoming atmosphere and pleasing ambience, high levels of comfort and guest care, and attractive surroundings enhanced by thoughtful design and attention to detail

STAR QUALITY GUIDE FOR

HOTELS, GUEST HOUSES AND FARMHOUSES

SELF-CATERING ACCOMMODATION
(Cottages, Apartments, Houses)

CARAVAN HOLIDAY HOME PARKS
(Holiday Parks, Touring Parks, Camping Parks)

★★★★★ *Exceptional quality*
★★★★ *Excellent quality*
★★★ *Very good quality*
★★ *Good quality*
★ *Fair to good quality*

In England, Scotland and Wales, all graded properties are inspected annually by Tourist Authority trained Assessors.

•• *Some Useful Guidance for Guests and Hosts* ••

Every year literally thousands of holidays, short breaks and overnight stops are arranged through our guides, the vast majority without any problems at all. In a handful of cases, however, difficulties do arise about bookings, which often could have been prevented from the outset.

It is important to remember that when accommodation has been booked, both parties – guests and hosts – have entered into a form of contract. We hope that the following points will provide helpful guidance.

GUESTS:

• When enquiring about accommodation, be as precise as possible. Give exact dates, numbers in your party and the ages of any children.

• State the number and type of rooms wanted and also what catering you require – bed and breakfast, full board etc. Make sure that the position about evening meals is clear – and about pets, reductions for children or any other special points.

• Read our reviews carefully to ensure that the proprietors you are going to contact can supply what you want. Ask for a letter confirming all arrangements, if possible.

• If you have to cancel, do so as soon as possible. Proprietors do have the right to retain deposits and under certain circumstances to charge for cancelled holidays if adequate notice is not given and they cannot re-let the accommodation.

HOSTS:

• Give details about your facilities and about any special conditions. Explain your deposit system clearly and arrangements for cancellations, charges etc. and whether or not your terms include VAT.

• If for any reason you are unable to fulfil an agreed booking without adequate notice, you may be under an obligation to arrange suitable alternative accommodation or to make some form of compensation.

While every effort is made to ensure accuracy, we regret that FHG Publications cannot accept responsibility for errors, omissions or misrepresentations in our entries or any consequences thereof. Prices in particular should be checked because we go to press early. We will follow up complaints but cannot act as arbiters or agents for either party.

OTHER FHG TITLES FOR 2005

FHG Publications have a large range of attractive holiday accommodation guides for all kinds of holiday opportunities throughout Britain. They also make useful gifts at any time of year. Our guides are available in most bookshops and larger newsagents but we will be happy to post you a copy direct if you have any difficulty. POST FREE for addresses in the UK. We will also post abroad but have to charge separately for post or freight.

SELF-CATERING HOLIDAYS ☐
in Britain
Over 1000 addresses throughout for self-catering and caravans
in Britain.

The original
Farm Holiday Guide to COAST & COUNTRY HOLIDAYS in England, ☐
Scotland, Wales and Channel Islands. Board, Self-catering, Caravans/Camping, Activity Holidays.

BRITAIN'S BEST HOLIDAYS ☐
A quick-reference general guide for all kinds of holidays.

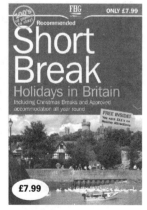

PETS WELCOME! ☐
The original and unique guide for holidays for pet owners and their pets.

Recommended
COUNTRY HOTELS ☐
of Britain
Including Country Houses, for the discriminating.

Recommended
SHORT BREAK HOLIDAYS IN BRITAIN ☐
"Approved" accommodation for quality bargain breaks.